sport
diver
manual

advanced open
water activities

volume II

NOTE

Any limits on activities mentioned in this manual are strictly general guidelines and should not be construed to be rules for sport diving regardless of experience level. All persons should evaluate their own capabilities and their own special circumstances which make their limits and parameters different.

International Standard Book Number 0-88487-054-5

First Edition © 1979 Jeppesen Sanderson, Inc.
8025 East 40th Avenue
Denver, Colorado USA 80207
First Printing March 1979
Second Printing March 1980

RE314750B

foreword

Open water diving is aptly named. The number of experiences you can have in the spectacular underwater world is as "wide open" as the ocean itself. Advanced open water training enhances these experiences and gives you the chance to have more of them. How, you might ask?

First of all, the information presented allows you to be a more competent and safe diver. Advanced open water training can also help increase confidence in your basic diving abilities, no matter what environmental conditions you encounter. Finally, the training in areas of limited visibility and boat diving, for example, naturally broadens the spectrum of diving spots you can enjoy.

Advanced open water activities education begins with the same tools of instruction as basic diver training — the manual and workbook. In fact, the Sport Diver Advanced Open Water Activities Kit has been designed as a companion to the Sport Diver Open Water Certification Kit, enabling both aspiring and experienced sport divers to have the most thorough and complete diving education possible. The novice student can refer to the advanced kit to gain the information needed to become a confident open water diver. The experienced student may find it beneficial to review basic diving material as given in the certification kit.

The manual and workbook are designed to supplement both classroom and open water sessions, held under the guidance of a qualified instructor. First, the subject is studied in the manual; then the corresponding section in the workbook is completed. The workbook contains self-study exercises designed to focus attention on practical problem-solving techniques. Advanced open water skills are discussed in the manual, but specific instruction techniques are left up to the instructor.

The manual is divided into eight parts:

Part I — Equipment Techniques — Shows how to make equipment work for the diver.

Part II — Specialized Equipment — Tells how to select equipment for special diving environments.

Part III — Boat Diving — Gives procedures to use on big charter boats and how to use small boats for diving.

Part IV — Underwater Navigation — Shows how to use navigation and the compass to save time, air, and energy.

Part V — Limited Visibility Diving — Covers night diving with its special requirements as well as low visibility situations.

Part VI — Diver Stress — Shows how the stress cycle begins and how to deal with stress above and below the water.

Part VII — Diver Rescue — Tells how to make a self rescue and a buddy rescue and discusses the situations surrounding them.

Part VIII — Deep Diving — Outlines procedures and special techniques for dives below 100 feet.

Remember, additional training can only bring you many more hours of diving ease and satisfaction.

contents

PART I
equipment
techniques

introduction

Diving is an equipment-intensive sport. It is impossible to dive without it: the mask, snorkel, buoyancy control device, tank, regulator, fins, various gauges, and other items are the diver's underwater life support system. No matter how experienced a diver may be, dives need to be made with complete and proper equipment. A diver is not safe just because he or she can breathe underwater. Under optimum conditions, in shallow water, it may be possible to make some dives with minimum equipment, but to be comfortable and safe, the diver needs to prepare for the unexpected.

All the equipment in the world will not make a diver safe unless it is of excellent quality. Luckily, the days of diving with a two-hose regulator without non-return valves; a narrow, corrugated snorkel; flimsy fins; tank harness made of webbing; gardening gloves; and other similar equipment are gone. Valuable equipment improvements, as well as new equipment designs appear so frequently that the diver just has no excuse for hanging onto old, unreliable standbys.

Yet even the finest diving equipment is not maintenance-free. Divers, like many people in other activities may assume equipment should simply work correctly and they are often quick to blame others for any malfunction. However, equipment failure is rarely a problem, because today's equipment is carefully manufactured, refined, and dependable. Most diving accidents can be traced to poor equipment maintenance, misuse, and misunderstanding of equipment.

The situations you encounter as an advanced diver require you to have more knowledge than you may have had as a basic diver about how your equipment functions, plus any modifications or adjustments needed for different situations, and potential problems. When you master your equipment, your advanced diving career becomes filled with pleasurable and memorable, rather than hair-raising underwater experiences.

overview
of equipment,
information equipment,
general maintenance

Diving equipment, as you know, can be broken down into several categories: equipment which helps vision, equipment which lets you move, equipment which sustains warmth, buoyancy control equipment, and information equipment.

Unless you can see, there is virtually no reason to dive, so the mask becomes the first essential piece of equipment. Next, the snorkel lets you breathe comfortably at the surface. The fins provide the propulsion needed to move easily through the water. All this allows you to stay underwater for extended periods, which can create discomfort, so you need a wet suit for protection. However, when the suit enters the picture, you become positively buoyant. To offset this, you need a weight belt and some kind of buoyancy control device. The buoyancy control device allows you to adjust for the decrease in the suit's buoyancy when you dive at depth.

To stay at depths comfortably for extended periods requires a tank, regulator, and the equipment to attach them to your body. Longer bottom times bring up another problem — extended exposure to pressure. To avoid any difficulties because of this, you need information equipment. Information equipment tells you how long you have been down, how deep you are, and which direction you are going.

This basic equipment is fundamental to your safety; to dive with anything less is unwise. This material is intended to give you information beyond what you received in basic diver training on equipment fit and maintenance. Selection of some equipment will be reviewed because you may want to replace or add equipment for certain advanced diving activities.

MASK, SNORKEL, AND FINS

During your basic training and from your subsequent diving experiences, you received an understanding of the most basic diving tools — the mask, snorkel, and fins. However, there are a few pointers that can help you more effectively use these and avoid future problems.

MASK FIT

Mask fit is very important. Leakage or discomfort occurs when your mask does not fit. To avoid both problems, be sure the mask, when laid lightly on your face, touches everywhere and the seal provides a comfortable contact on your face. This is important when you wear the mask for long periods, because the seal creates pressure which, in turn, can cause discomfort. Adjust the strap so the mask fits evenly on your

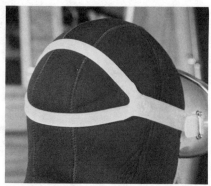

Fig. 1-1 Strap Placement

face and the split strap is spaced evenly above and below the crown of your head, as shown in figure 1-1. The mask should be tight enough to stay on, but not so tight as to cause an uncomfortable squeeze.

MASK MAINTENANCE

The most frequent mask problems include fogging, rotting, and slipping straps. The best solution to lens fogging is prevention. This includes cleaning the mask lens thoroughly with toothpaste or liquid dishwashing soap before you use it the first time. This removes the silicone the manufacturer places on the mask to protect it during shipping and assures that the lens begins clean. Then, coat the lens with a chemical wetting agent, not saliva. While saliva does work, the wetting agent leaves a chemical film on the lens surface which keeps the lens clearer than saliva.

The best way to prevent rotting is to coat the rubber parts of the mask, except the strap, with spray silicone or some kind of rubber preservative. (See figure 1-2.) The strap does not need to be sprayed because silicone is slippery and could cause the strap to unbuckle unexpectedly. This protective measure on the other rubber parts of the mask prevents ozone from reaching the material and keeps it supple and durable.

Delay breakage of the retainer buckles, strap, lens, and frame by inspecting the mask and packing it carefully in the gear bag. Watch for corrosion as well. Keep buckles clean by washing them after use. It is not completely possible to keep the strap and lens from breaking, but you can replace these parts easily in quality masks.

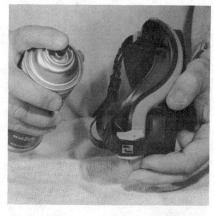

Fig. 1-2 Protecting Rubber on Mask

If your mask has a purge valve, check it by inhaling to hold the mask on your face and exhaling to force air out as you hold the mask with your hands. If the valve is stuck open, the mask will not stay on your face when you inhale, and if it is stuck shut, you will not be able to exhale. If water seeps into your mask during a dive, the purge valve may have become weak. In this case, replace the valve.

SNORKEL FIT

The snorkel should be adjusted so when you look straight down, the snorkel is as nearly vertical as possible. (See figure 1-3.) The mouthpiece should not press too hard on either your upper or lower gums as this can irritate your mouth. If the mouthpiece is uncomfortable, you can sand the edges, trim it with scissors, or, in some cases, replace the mouthpiece.

SNORKEL MAINTENANCE

The greatest snorkel problems come primarily from wear. To prevent deterioration from ozone, keep the snorkel lubricated with a rubber preservative such as silicone. Regularly wash the snorkel with water and clean it once in a while with a mouthwash, disinfectant, or soap. Do not forget to check the snorkel keeper for wear.

The longer the snorkel, the greater the breathing resistance. If this is a problem you encounter, you can often shorten the snorkel. Just make sure

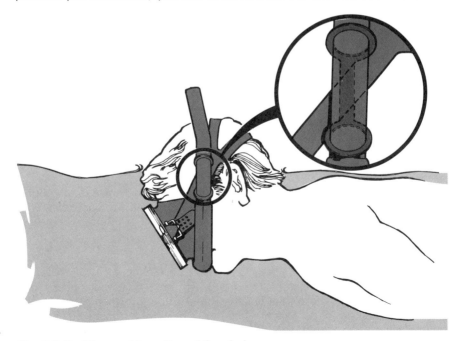

Fig. 1-3 Position and Location of Snorkel

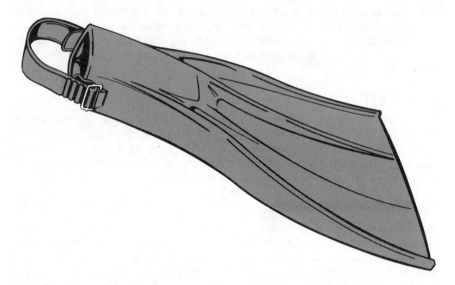

Fig. 1-4 Strap Modification

the end is still above the surface of the water when you use it. You should always replace the brightly colored band by attaching bright tape to the top of the tube. If your snorkel did not come with this band, be sure to use bright-colored tape, so you will be easier to see in the water.

FIN FIT

Your fins should fit tight enough so they do not slide on your feet, but at the same time, they should be loose enough so you do not experience cramps. If you have adjustable straps, set them snugly enough so they hold, but not so tight as to make your toes rub against the end of the foot pockets. Turn the straps so they are threaded through the buckle system with the loose ends on the inside. (See figure 1-4.) Then wrap the loose ends with black electrical tape so they are secure.

Fins sometimes come from the manufacturer with small pieces of rubber, called mold splashings protruding from drain holes and foot pockets. Trim these off with a sharp, thin knife or razor so they do not interfere with how the fins fit and also, to streamline the fins.

FIN MAINTENANCE

A limited number of things can go wrong with fins. Adjustable straps may break or heel pockets of full-foot fins may break through. When a heel pocket breaks, you can no longer use the fins, however, when a strap breaks, you can replace it. You should watch for wear and check the straps, as shown in figure 1-5. If you notice marks, replace the straps before they break.

Fig. 1-5 Wear on Heel Strap

Because buckles sometimes separate and become loose, tap the ends with a hammer to flatten and secure them, as shown in figure 1-6. Another thing to look for is corrosion of both the buckle and pin mechanism. It is a good idea to carry an extra buckle in your repair kit so your dive is not ruined if you lose or break a buckle.

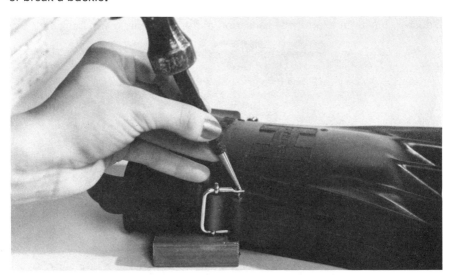

Fig. 1-6 Securing Fin Buckles

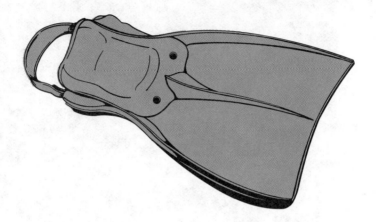

Fig. 1-7 Holes Drilled in Foot Pocket

Fin pockets filled with sand are an inconvenience. You can minimize this problem by drilling holes into the top sole of the foot pockets. The holes should be no larger than one-fourth inch to be effective. (See figure 1-7.)

WEIGHT BELT

ADJUSTMENT

Two considerations for the weight belt are placement of weight and type of buckle. The weights should be set just slightly forward of the center of the hips, as shown in figure 1-8. This lets you rest facing forward more easily and reduces, to a great extent, the sensation of the tank pulling you backwards.

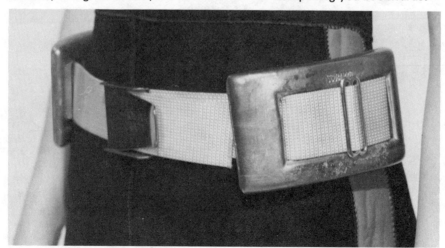

Fig. 1-8 Location of Hip Weights

Fig. 1-9 Non-Slip Clip

Fig. 1-10 Securing Weights

To prevent weights from sliding off your belt when you are taking the belt off or putting it on, use non-slip clips, as shown in figure 1-9. You must remove the clips when you change weights. Another way to keep weights in place is to twist the strap once after it goes through one slot in the weight and then pass the strap as you would normally through the next slot. (See figure 1-10.) Do this to the first and last weights on the belt.

The buckle should be the quick-release type. Two types are available: the wire frame and standard metal buckles. The buckle on your weight belt should be different from any other buckle on the rest of your equipment. This helps you to not confuse buckles in an emergency requiring the ditching of weights.

MAINTENANCE

The buckle and strap ends need attention. Avoid damage to the buckle so it does not become bent and thereby useless. Wash it regularly to keep it free of corrosion. Adjust the strap ends so there is about six inches of belt remaining when you are wearing both wet suit and weight belt. Nylon strap ends should be kept free of frayed material by heating them with an open flame to seal the tips of the material and then applying a light coat of wet suit cement, as shown in figure 1-11. Another way to prevent fraying is to dip the ends in liquid vinyl.

BUOYANCY CONTROL DEVICES

There is a wide variety of buoyancy control devices available, from the small CO_2 vest, designed for the skin diver, to the buoyancy control packs and wraparound designs. The small CO_2 vest is not adequate nor is it really intended to be used by scuba divers. There are larger CO_2 units with the same general characteristics of the smaller skin diving units, but most of these have large oral inflation tubes which make them suitable for scuba diving as well.

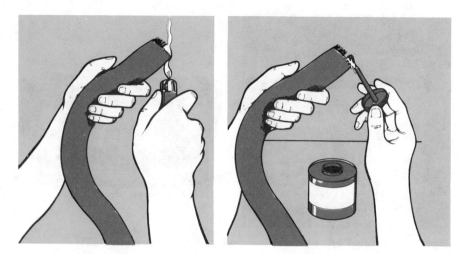

Fig. 1-11 Modifying Weight Belt Strap

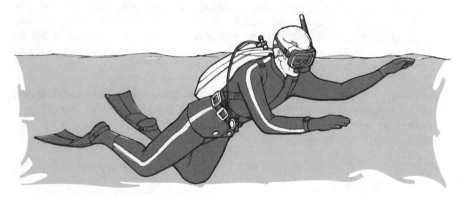

Fig. 1-12 Buoyancy Control Pack

The large, front-mounted vests with over 30 pounds of flotation are adequate for scuba diving. However, it is often difficult to swim facedown in them and they may not be as comfortable as the newer wraparound models. Buoyancy control packs, as shown in figure 1-12, are designed especially for scuba diving. They have large flotation capabilities. The wraparound buoyancy control devices worn like jackets improve your stability and are designed strictly for scuba diving. (See figure 1-13.)

Fig. 1-13 Wraparound Buoyancy Compensators

Fig. 1-14 Proper Strap Adjustment

FIT

The adjustment of straps and placement of buckles are crucial to how your buoyancy control device will fit. The most important adjustment for the front-mounted vest is with the straps. The waist strap must be tight enough to keep the vest from riding up when inflated. It is best to adjust the waist strap when the vest is inflated. If there is a buckle, you should be able to open and close it with one hand. Once the waist strap has been properly adjusted, adjust the crotch strap so it is snug. (See figure 1-14.) These straps prevent an inflated vest from riding up and creating discomfort in the crotch or around the neck.

The backpack of the buoyancy control pack must be properly adjusted for fit. Correct adjustment keeps the unit from riding up off your back during inflation. Be sure the shoulder and waist straps are properly adjusted and fit tightly. The backpack buckle should fasten on the side away from the weight belt buckle. This prevents confusion between buckles.

Wraparound buoyancy compensators need less adjustment, except for the front buckle which should fasten near the middle of your waist, as shown in figure 1-15. A good fit is most important. They need to fit

Fig. 1-15 Buckle Position

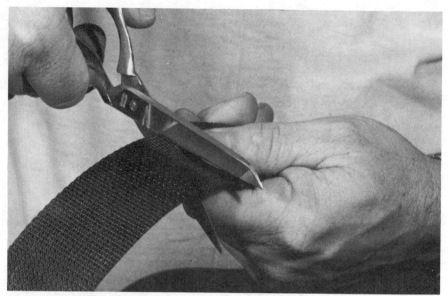

Fig. 1-16 Buoyancy Control Device Strap Modification

snug, yet still allow room for inflation and they should not be uncomfortable when inflated. The waist strap should be tight enough so the unit does not ride up excessively when you inflate it. Once you have adjusted the straps and have set the buckles exactly where you want them on any buoyancy control device, trim the excess material beyond the buckles and secure the loose ends with electrical tape, as shown in figure 1-16.

MAINTENANCE

Buoyancy control devices are very subject to wear and tear, primarily because they extend outward from your body even when partially inflated. The most troublesome wear is caused by punctures or abrasion but proper care and handling can prevent excess wear on this valuable piece of diving equipment.

Salt water can damage both the exterior and interior of a buoyancy control device. Since a little water leaks into the vest when you use the oral inflator, you must rinse the interior. The best way to do this is to fill the vest with air, flood the interior with warm, fresh water, move the vest from side to side and top to bottom, and finally open the valve to let the water completely drain. Reinflate the device and hang it up so residual moisture can drain into the oral inflation hose.

To rinse a CO_2 cartridge, let the water inside the vest flow to the CO_2 mechanism. Then remove the cartridge and squeeze the vest to force the water out. You should do this only after you have tasted the water to make sure it is clean and salt-free. Salt buildup can corrode the CO_2 mechanism.

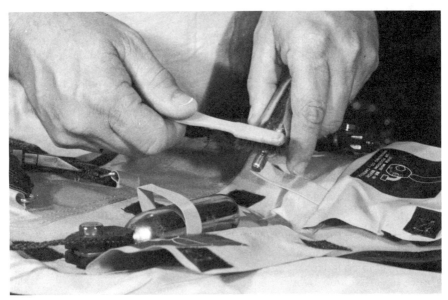

Fig. 1-17 CO2 Cartridge Maintenance

All mechanical parts should be washed and sprayed with a silicone lubricant. You must also clean the threads on the neck of the bottle. (See figure 1-17.) Relubricate the threads with silicone grease before you put the cartridge back together.

TANK ADJUSTMENT

The height of the tank backpack and the pack adjustment are the most important items to check when adjusting your tank and pack. The height of the pack should be as shown in figure 1-18 and the pack should be set just low enough on the tank so there is room to place the filler yoke on the valve without readjusting the pack. When you put the assembled unit on, lift it high on your back and make the shoulder straps tight enough to hold the pack and tank securely in place. At the same time, allow sufficient room to move your arms. Finally, pull the waist strap so it is snug and secure.

Backpacks are designed to allow for a permanent adjustment. Once you properly adjust shoulder straps, set the buckle to hook on the left side, around the waist. Then you can remove excess material and secure the ends with black electrical tape.

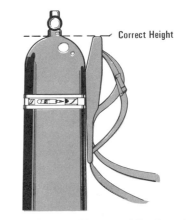

Fig. 1-18 Correct Height of Backpack

MAINTENANCE

Regular, thorough tank maintenance means having tanks inspected internally at least once a year. But they also should be inspected anytime there is obvious damage, such as rust on the exterior or any sign of cuts, gouges, or pits. It is recommended that rental cylinders or those undergoing heavy use be inspected every three months. Tanks should also be inspected each time they are completely drained during use, because a completely drained tank can allow water to enter through the regulator. Brand new tanks, less than six weeks old, have been completely destroyed by salt water entering the tank. They should also be inspected if the air has any odor or taste.

Tanks are required by federal law to be hydrostatically tested every five years. You should also have your tanks hydrostatically tested anytime you see obvious visual damage. Several problems, as shown in figure 1-19, can occur to tanks.

Tanks are quite rugged and the probability of damage that may remove a tank from service in fresh water is rare. The types of damage that can cause a tank to deteriorate over a period of time can be avoided by thoroughly rinsing the tank's exterior with fresh water after every use. Continual exposure to salt water requires this rinsing process to avoid structural tank damage.

Backpack maintenance includes maintaining the buckles and straps just as you do those on the weight belt. The strap ends need to be prepared exactly as the weight belt to avoid frayed ends.

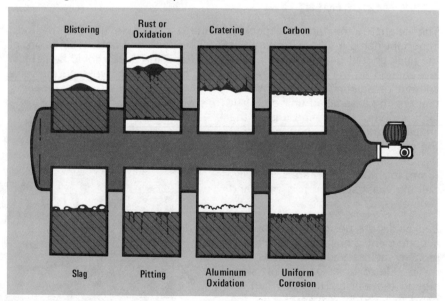

Fig. 1-19 Tank Problems

REGULATOR
SELECTION

Single-hose regulators are manufactured primarily with one of two designs. Both first and second stages can be either *balanced* or *unbalanced*. Unbalanced regulators have an increase in breathing resistance when decreased tank pressure (usually 300 to 600 psi) causes a difference in how well the first stage opens and closes. It requires more effort at the end of the dive than at the beginning of the dive to open the first stage for inhalation. Less-expensive, unbalanced regulators also use other less sophisticated designs and lower quality material than the more expensive regulators. While these are not inadequate, they are not of the quality you find in balanced regulators. Unbalanced regulators are strictly for people who dive occasionally under good conditions or they sometimes can be used as backup units.

If you want dependable, smooth regulator operation and intend to use this equipment frequently, choose a higher-cost, balanced regulator. This design functions with minimum breathing effort and at maximum efficiency, providing little breathing resistance at all tank pressures.

MAINTENANCE

Careful regulator maintenance is very necessary to prevent rust and salt corrosion from damaging this delicate piece of equipment. The moving parts inside the regulator are built close together and do not adapt to foreign material obstructing any passages. All parts are also made of stainless steel, brass, teflon, nylon, rubber, or plastic, which are all rust-resistant materials. The only way rust can enter a regulator is from the tank. Salt entering the first stage can do much harm if you do not rinse this stage thoroughly. When the salt dries, it forms crystals which can build up, cause friction between the moving parts, thus causing breathing resistance, and in some cases, it can stop the air flow.

Another major cause of leaks in the first stage is faulty or unlubricated "O" rings. This can also cause leaks in the low pressure hose at the connections, or it could be that the hose needs to be tightened in these areas. Leaks or water in the second stage may stem from either a faulty demand diaphragm or exhaust diaphragm, as shown in figure 1-20, or bent seat on the exhaust diaphragm port, as shown in figure 1-21.

Other problems, such as adjustments or any overhauling of the internal mechanism in either the first or second stage, in addition to the problems just discussed, absolutely require that you take the regulator in for professional service. Regulator repair is beyond the realm of most sport divers. In any event, regulators that are used on a regular basis should be serviced at least once a year and more often if they are used heavily in the ocean. It is vital for your regulator to function at peak efficiency at all times.

Fig. 1-20 Faulty Exhaust
           Diaphragm on Regulator

Fig. 1-21 Bent Seat on Exhaust
           Diaphragm

The more conscientious you are about caring for your regulator in the first place, the less professional maintenance it will need and the less money you will have to spend on this maintenance. Good regulator care actually begins with using it properly underwater.

Divers can be quite a spectacle underwater when wearing basic gear, but this is amplified if various hoses are floating at different angles from your body. (See figure 1-22.) This is not only an eyesore and a hindrance to your swimming ability, it can also be hazardous. If not secured somehow to your body, the various hoses coming off the first stage of the regulator; the octopus second stage, submersible pressure gauge, mechanical inflator for the buoyancy control device, and your own second stage when you are snorkeling; may become entangled in rocks, kelp, and lines. This can damage the hoses and the regulator itself. If you are passing through heavy surf, it is possible for instruments attached to the hoses to fly up and hit you, causing possible injury.

It is very important to secure the octopus second stage to keep it from free-flowing, becoming fouled with sand or mud, or creating confusion in an emergency. Stow the octopus regulator near your chest so you or your buddy has access to it during an out-of-air situation and so you can reach it easily to use if your second stage regulator should malfunction.

Fig. 1-22 Diving Spectacle

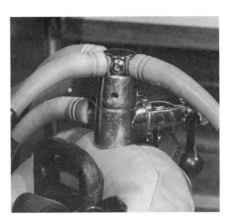

Fig. 1-23 Bulge in Second-Stage   Fig. 1-24 Commercial Stress
          Regulator Hose   Sleeves

Another reason for keeping your hoses under control is to reduce drag on the hoses. This can weaken the area where hoses are attached to the first stage. A good way to see if this has happened is to bend the hose at about a 45-degree angle, as shown in figure 1-23, and if you notice a bulge, change the hose as soon as possible. Otherwise, the hose could rupture, which shuts off the supply of air from the tank and fills the hose and regulator with water. You can prevent much of the strain placed on hoses by using commercial stress sleeves. (See figure 1-24.)

At the end of your dive, you should not leave the regulator on a tank that is standing upright, because this also puts a strain on the hoses. When you remove the regulator from the tank, blow the dust cap dry orally or dry it with a towel. If you use tank air to dry the dust cap, be careful to not blow water into the regulator inlet. When the cap has been thoroughly dried, place it over the high pressure inlet of the first stage and tighten the yoke screw for a good seal. Be sure not to damage the "O" ring or the dust cap itself by tightening the yoke screw too much.

One type of dust cap is plastic with a solid core in the center and an "O" ring on the bottom for a seal. The "O" ring provides a proper seal. Once the dust cap is in place, rinse the first stage with fresh, warm water. Flush the ports for about two minutes to dilute any salt and to wash out any sand that may have accumulated inside. Since sand collects even more easily in the large chamber of the second stage regulator, rinse it for about three minutes. Hold the exhaust tee at the lowest point and let water flow into the mouthpiece and out the exhaust tee, as shown in figure 1-25. Do not push the purge button when you are doing this ás sand and salt crystals may enter the valve and go through the hose into the first stage, causing regulator malfunction.

Always lay the regulator down rather than hanging it by the yoke. (See figure 1-26.) When the regulator is allowed to hang, the hoses bend slightly and the

Fig. 1-25 Flushing the Mouthpiece

Fig. 1-26 Regulator Handling

weight of the second stage breaks down the hose fibers. Also, be careful not to coil the hoses tightly during storage; this can also weaken the hoses. Keep the regulator out of direct sunlight, because too much sunlight can cause rapid deterioration of the rubber. Instead, store it in a dark, cool, dry place.

Using silicone to lubricate your regulator hoses and working metal parts to prevent malfunctions has several drawbacks:

1. Although silicone is considered nontoxic, if used in large quantities, it could become toxic at greater than average depths.
2. Silicone can become gummy if sprayed inside the regulator.
3. It makes the edge of the diaphragm slippery and when silicone goes through the rubber pores and into the clamping areas of the diaphragm, it is possible for the diaphragm to become unseated.
4. It causes rubber, such as the low pressure diaphragm and the exhale valve, to warp.
5. Sand clings to areas sprayed with silicone.

Silicone can be effective for smooth regulator function if it is used properly. Only qualified persons should use silicone when the regulator is undergoing regular maintenance.

KNIFE

The type of knife you own depends strictly on how you intend to use it. Carry the knife where it is easiest to reach. There are several spots favored by divers, the lower leg, thigh, and the hip. If the knife is worn on the lower leg around the calf, place it on the inside of the leg, as shown in figure 1-27, so it will not get caught on any objects, such as kelp or fish lines. If you wear the knife on your thigh, attach it either with a knife pocket or by fasteners. This allows for additional comfort and ease of attachment without the restriction and insecurity of the straps. When your knife becomes dull, do not hone it, rather sharpen it with a fine file.

INFORMATION EQUIPMENT

So many subtle, yet critical things happen to the body under pressure, that it is necessary to monitor physical changes while diving. The increased pressure causes the body to absorb more gases and if you stay down longer and dive deeper, you absorb more gases. As a result, you must determine how long you are down and how deep you go, while also monitoring your air supply and staying aware of the water temperature.

At this stage in your training, you should be familiar with the equipment that provides underwater orientation and which can keep you within safe diving depths. Knowing that your submersible pressure gauge, depth gauge, compass, watch, and decompression computer are all working properly because of regular maintenance can certainly make your dives much more comfortable and relaxing. You will not have to wonder if you have exceeded your depth limits, because you know your depth gauge is accurately calibrated and you will be assured your compass is guiding you in the right direction, because you have regularly checked it and treated it as you would any fine instrument.

SUBMERSIBLE PRESSURE GAUGE

There should be no question about why it is important to continuously watch your air supply. To run out of air underwater not only marks you as a poor diver, but is also dangerous. There is simply no excuse with the excellent gauges available, to ever unknowingly run out of air. The only accurate way to monitor your air consumption rate is with a standard submersible pressure gauge. (See figure 1-28.) It is generally available in one quality level and therefore requires little note, except that some pressure gauges have certain options which allow you to keep track of bottom time and, in some cases, depth.

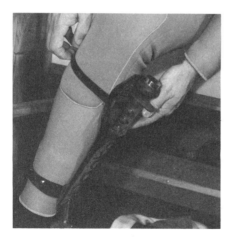

Fig. 1-27 Proper Placement of Knife   Fig. 1-28 Submersible Pressure Gauge

Fig. 1-29 Faulty High Pressure Hose

Fig. 1-30 "J" Valve Reserve Lever

Maintenance

The most common problems with pressure gauges are leaks, generally caused by dried "O" rings or damage from rough use. Cleaning, replacement, and lubrication at a qualified repair facility usually corrects these problems. You should also take your gauge in for repair if you notice any moisture under the lens or if you suspect that salt water and other contaminants have entered the internal mechanism. Qualified personnel can also make sure all connections in the pressure gauge are tight.

If you notice bubbles coming from the hose, as shown in figure 1-29, replace it. This hose should be given the same treatment as the low pressure hose of the second stage regulator. Either attach the hose to one piece of equipment with a strap or tuck it under your vest. This also protects the lens face and the delicate calibration of the mechanism. You may also want to use a protective rubber housing for the gauge.

The pressure gauge lens receives the most wear. Scratches and a certain amount of the nicks and cuts can be polished with a fine, mild abrasive to let you see the pressure scale clearly. Underwater, scratches are not a problem as the water fills them in.

RESERVE SYSTEMS

The alternatives to the pressure gauge are reserve systems. They are not viable alternatives however, because they should be used as a backup to the pressure gauge. There are two types of reserve systems. The constant reserve is a mechanical lever, as shown in figure 1-30, which operates by spring tension, allowing air to pass through down to a preset level of 300 to 600 psi. When the pressure reaches the preset level, the spring moves a pin into the air passage and greatly restricts the air supply. At that point, the reserve spring can be mechanically bypassed to provide an additional 300 to 600 psi of air. One of the problems of using this system alone is that 300 to 600 psi, under certain diving circumstances, may not be sufficient to allow a proper, safe ascent. Another type of reserve is the audible reserve which activates on low air pressure. It, too, serves to back up the submersible pressure gauge.

DEPTH GAUGE

The reasons for keeping track of depth have been explored at great length. The increased gas absorption and the need to prevent too much gas from entering the body at depth have been well established, as have the types of depth gauges. What has not been clearly defined is exactly how these gauges work.

Of the three basic designs of depth gauges, the capillary, bourdon tube, and diaphragm, the capillary gauge mechanism is the simplest. The capillary gauge, as shown in figure 1-31, works on the basic principle of Boyle's law. It has an air-filled tube sealed at one end. The air inside the tube compresses as the water pressure increases. When you descend to 33 feet, the ambient pressure doubles and therefore the volume is cut in half, as shown in figure 1-32. This natural law makes it possible to actually measure the percentage of pressure increase and apply that to the length of the tube to get the precise readings of depth down to approximately 33 feet. From 33 feet on, they are progressively less accurate and more difficult to read because the graduations are closer together.

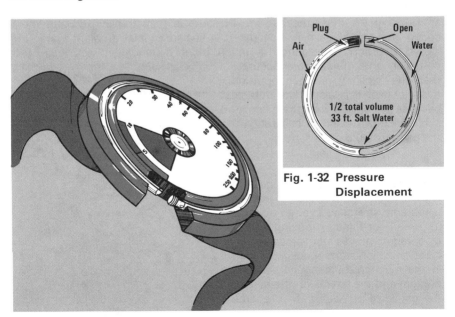

Fig. 1-32 Pressure Displacement

Fig. 1-31 Capillary Depth Gauge

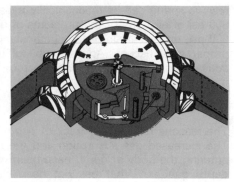

Fig. 1-33 Open Bourdon Tube Depth   Fig. 1-34 Closed Bourdon Tube Depth
          Gauge   Gauge

Both the open and closed bourdon tube depth gauges, as shown in figures 1-33 and 1-34, work on the same principle. Ambient pressure is transmitted to the basic mechanism of the gauge, called the C spring, which is a hollow spring in the shape of a "C." This transfer of pressure straightens the spring. This motion is then transferred to the dial.

The difference between the open and closed bourdon tube is that water passes through the opening in the side of the open bourdon tube gauge to straighten the spring. In the closed bourdon tube depth gauge, surrounding pressure from all directions is transmitted from outside to the liquid surrounding the inner mechanism. Pressure is then transmitted into the C spring and on to the dial. Because it is sealed against ambient water, the closed bourdon tube gauge is much more dependable, less subject to corrosion and much more accurate than the capillary or open bourdon tube gauges. It is also more durable because the oil cushions the gears inside which protects the calibration if the gauge should be dropped.

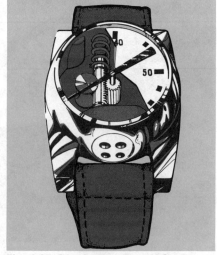

The diaphragm depth gauge, as shown in figure 1-35, has a diaphragm stretched over an opening in the air-filled housing. The diaphragm moves as pressure increases, which starts a chain reaction in the mechanism between the diaphragm and the needle on the face of the gauge. The needle then records the depth on the scale. This is perhaps the most accurate depth gauge.

Fig. 1-35 Diaphragm Depth Gauge

One other depth gauge is a combination of the oil-filled bourdon tube and capillary gauges. Divers who make deep dives can benefit the most from this gauge because the combination of two different scales gives accurate readings at all depths.

Maintenance

Maintenance for depth gauges primarily involves thorough rinsing to prevent corrosion, however, all three types of gauges have slightly different rinsing methods. On the capillary gauge, you must first carefully remove the gauge tube and connection insert, flush these with fresh water, and run a pipe cleaner through the tube. When you reassemble the device, make sure the insert which holds the two ends of the tube faces the left end of the tube and has the notched side up. If this is not replaced properly, the gauge will register backwards.

Since the open bourdon tube depth gauge has a very small opening in the case, it is subject to corrosion and plugging from impurities and you need sufficient water pressure to clean it. Hydraulic dental devices do a good job. Let the gauge register to 30 feet several times while you rinse the gauge. You can also submerge the pressure gauge in water while you are rinsing the port. Another method for eliminating corrosion is to immerse the gauge in white vinegar for a short time, rinse thoroughly with clear water, and relubricate with a light lubricant, such as silicone. Do not leave your depth gauge in the vinegar too long, because it is a mild acid and could cause damage. It is only necessary to rinse the exterior of oil-filled bourdon tube and diaphragm depth gauges with water because they have no open ports. Since all but the capillary gauge are affected by heat and cold, protect depth gauges from temperature extremes.

The greatest wear comes from abrasion and scuffing of the lens cover. Polishing with a mild abrasive removes the scuffs to a large extent. You should have the gauge regularly checked for accurate calibration, but if you discover discrepancy in accuracy or any kind of internal damage at any time, take the depth gauge in for professional repair.

COMPASS

The underwater compass comes in three basic models: the small wristband compass that fits on the watch or depth gauge, and the wrist compass in either the top- or side-reading styles. The wrist models generally fit into a console or can be used individually. The higher-quality wrist models are much more desirable for underwater navigation. Watchband compasses are for appearance and general direction control. The other compass styles allow more precise navigation.

Maintenance

Basic compass maintenance should deal with loose or sticky components or damage to the compass card. In all cases, keep the exterior clean and well-

Fig. 1-36 Transporting Compass

Fig. 1-37 Instrument Panel or Console

lubricated with silicone grease, as opposed to silicone spray. You should also transport it carefully, as shown in figure 1-36. The compass is a delicate instrument and will not stand up to heavy abuse. Damage to the compass card usually requires in-shop service.

CONSOLE

One answer to the profusion of gauges that hang from a diver's body is the instrument panel, also called a console. (See figure 1-37.) This device encloses the submersible pressure gauge, depth gauge, compass, and sometimes the decompression meter in one unit mounted on the pressure gauge hose. An option to this is to attach the depth gauge on the back of the pressure gauge. There are units made especially for this purpose. The other gauges are worn separately on the wrist or in pockets. Because the metal in other gauges may affect the magnetism of the compass, it works more accurately when you wear it separate from other gauges.

Both the console and pressure gauge assembly should be secured near the front of the buoyancy control device and under the left arm to permit easy scanning of the gauges. This position keeps the console from becoming entangled or getting in the way. (See figure 1-38.)

DIVE WATCH

If your diving watch is pressure-proof beyond whatever depth you intend to go, it should cause you no problems. Higher-priced watches have such features as a mineral crystal, a higher-quality interior mechanism, and significantly greater durability than other watches. They can withstand more abuse and, of course, have increased accuracy.

Fig. 1-38 Proper Placement of Console

Fig. 1-39 Setting Desired Time **Fig. 1-40 Remembering Bottom Time**

The most crucial part of the watch is the bezel. You can use it in two ways: either set the amount of time you wish to be down, as shown in figure 1-39, or set the indicator at the time you go down and keep track of how long you stay underwater, as shown in figure 1-40.

Other styles of watches, called *chronograph* watches have lapse-time counters which are activated as you enter the water and actually record the time spent underwater. (See figure 1-41.) Another method of measuring bottom time is with a unit which activates on pressure once you reach five to eight feet. It remains on as long as it is under pressure and turns off when you return to shallow water. (See figure 1-42.)

Fig. 1-41 Chronograph Watch **Fig. 1-42 Dive Timer**

Fig.1-43 Proper Band for Diving Watch   Fig. 1-44 Thermometer

The best watchband to have is one that passes through both retaining pins. (See figure 1-43.) Bands which attach separately to each side of the watch are too easy to lose underwater.

THERMOMETER

To prevent hypothermia and to let you know what thickness of wet suit to use, it is important that you monitor water temperatures. This becomes a simple process with the small watchband thermometer, shown in figure 1-44.

GENERAL EQUIPMENT CARE

There are several general hints for regular maintenance that can greatly prolong the life of your equipment. Of course, you should always rinse your gear after every dive with clean, fresh, preferably lukewarm water. Since excessive heat can harm equipment, particulary equipment with rubber parts and pressurized mechanisms, keep it out of the sun as much as possible and store all pieces at a constant temperature away from polluted areas and electric engines. If you need to store your gear for a long time, seal each piece individually in plastic bags after making sure everything is dry.

Remember to take both your tank and regulator in for annual inspection, and more frequently if you detect any damage or breathing resistance. This tip is not limited to the tank and regulator alone. Anything other than the simplest of problems normally requires that you take the equipment to a professional repair person for proper maintenance. If you have difficulty with equipment modifications, such as arranging your fin straps, do not be timid; ask for help from your buddy, other divers, or the store where you purchased the equipment. Most divers have had the same difficulties at one time or another and all divers should know that the more than can be done to insure safety on a dive, the better.

PART II
specialized
equipment

introduction

For a long time, the only thing keeping people from enjoying the underwater world was lack of equipment. Today, fortunately, that is not the case. Once the basic equipment for seeing, breathing, and moving underwater was created, manufacturers proceeded quickly into not only improving the equipment, but also developing equipment which would let the diver do much more than descend, look around for awhile, and ascend. You might say these developments turned the *activity* of diving into a varied and unique *sport*.

Sport divers today can do everything from carrying on conversations beneath the surface to locating precious metals several feet below the ocean bottom. What is more, further advances in diving equipment are on the drawing boards with yet undreamed of fantastic devices for the future.

hypothermia, communication, extended dives, additional equipment

The learning process has several stages. The first is familiarity. Most information about diving equipment begins with familiarity and offers a little bit of knowledge about the equipment. At this stage, you may know, for example, that the body gets cold underwater and that it needs protection. You may even know how to protect it. But there may be a lack of real understanding about exactly what happens with equipment designed to protect you from the cold, how it works, and why the equipment is so important.

Our goal is to step to the next level of learning — understanding. This material discusses many of the same areas of equipment that have been discussed many times before, but it presents a new dimension at a level of understanding so you can make well-informed decisions about diving equipment, based on something more than familiarity.

HYPOTHERMIA

Hypothermia is a drop in the body's temperature. The word hypothermia comes from two Greek words: "hypo," meaning low and "therme," meaning heat, or low heat. The body functions at 98.6°F (37°C). Even when you "feel" cold, the core heat remains very close to that temperature, but it does not have to drop much before several dramatic changes happen. Just a few degrees drop in the actual core temperature can cause rather severe problems. A series of events takes place in the body and if they are not reversed, they can be quite serious and even cause death. Hypothermia underwater is potentially more serious than on land because water dissipates heat 25 times faster than air.

SYMPTOMS

At first, when you get cold, the blood from the extremities begins to move into the central or core part of the body to protect it and keep it warm and functioning. The first obvious signs of hypothermia are "goose bumps" on the skin and very light shivering or chill. Although this is certainly not a serious situation, it does indicate that the body is beginning to make changes to protect the core. At this point, the core heat remains stable, or nearly stable, and only the extremities are affected. If the cold continues, the body starts shivering violently to warm the muscles and blood. Once this happens,

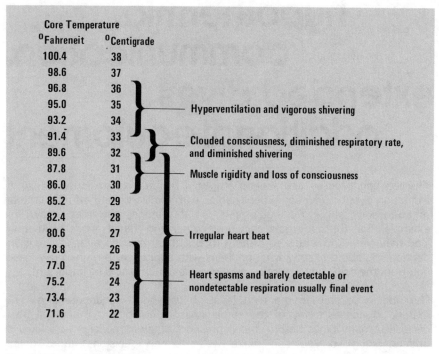

Fig. 2-1 Hypothermia Symptoms

the core heat has actually begun to drop. Figure 2-1 shows the levels of the core temperature in relation to hypothermia symptoms.

The blood pressure also drops lower than normal and the pulse is generally slow and often irregular at this time. It may be difficult to locate the pulse in the extremities because the blood vessels, in an effort to warm the blood, constrict. In this case, the best place for measuring the heart rate is in the neck at the carotid artery, or at the groin on a femoral artery.

Persons suffering from hypothermia vary in their levels of consciousness. As the core temperature goes down and nears 90°F (32°C), the consciousness becomes more and more clouded and loss of consciousness actually occurs between 86° to 90°F (30° to 32°C). Respiration is initially increased in the early stages of hypothermia, but as the core temperature falls below 92°F (33°C), the respiratory rate gradually goes down and at a low core temperature, respiration is very slow and often labored.

Shivering is a reflex mechanism the body uses to produce heat. It becomes increasingly vigorous and uncontrolled as the core temperature nears 95°F (35°C), but steadily diminishes between 90°F to 95°F (32°C to 35°C). Shivering is replaced by muscular rigidity by the time the temperature gets down to 86° to 90°F (30° to 32°C).

When a diver begins to shiver while involved in increased exercise, it means the exercise is drawing heat from the center of the body and moving it to the extremities. What actually happens is that as the extremities become cold from the heat loss and movement of blood into the core, they begin to hurt and become numb, but as you stimulate the extremities during exercise, you draw warm blood from the core. This steadily reduces the core temperature, which causes a more rapid loss of heat, as opposed to warming the body as is often believed.

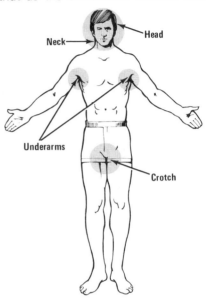

The areas of greatest heat loss, as shown in figure 2-2, are the head and neck, under the arms, and the groin region. These areas generally have less fatty tissue and, therefore, less protection. For a diver, these are areas of critical protection even in relatively warm water in excess of 75° to 80°F (24° to 26°C). These areas are the most vulnerable, so when they are protected, you are the most comfortable.

Fig. 2-2 Areas of Greatest Heat Loss

The hypothermia victim is normally pale and the skin feels very cold to the touch. In fact, the temperature of the skin is sometimes lowered to that of the water temperature around it. The pupils begin to dilate when the core temperature nears 92°F (32°C) and then are fully dilated and will not react, or barely react to light, when the core temperature gets to around 86°F (30°C).

TREATMENT AND PREVENTION

If you suspect that a diver has hypothermia, first give mouth-to-mouth artificial respiration, if the person is not breathing. Next, take the victim to a warm place as soon as possible and remove any constricting clothing or clothing that is wet or frozen. Wrap the victim in warm blankets or place the victim in a tub of *warm*, not hot, water. This provides a rapid rewarming process. Administer hot liquids by mouth if the victim is conscious. A person suffering from hypothermia should not be given alcohol. Dry the victim thoroughly if you used water for the warming process.

Besides diving in cold water, the consumption of alcohol contributes significantly to the rate and amount of body heat loss. Alcohol consumption initially decreases shivering because it increases the blood flow close to the skin's surface. That makes you feel warmer, but actually, heat loss from the body is accelerated because alcohol thins the blood and pulls it to the surface. While the exact effect of alcohol consumption on survival time in cold water has not been determined, there is little question that during any time of critical decision-making, anything that might impair your ability to think is undesirable. So alcohol should be avoided in connection with water activity.

It is vital to properly prepare for your particular diving conditions. Even if you generally function in a warm water environment, you are susceptible to significant body heat loss. Even 80°F (26°C) water can lower the body temperature to a point where serious results can take place. Because of this, you should carefully consider the kind of protection you use.

WET SUIT PROTECTION

You can immediately notice several very obvious things about a wet suit. It is clearly meant for protection from the cold; but why it is needed and how it does this is not clearly understood. If the core temperature begins to drop even in warm water, it affects your ability to think rationally. It may not cause a significant alteration in the thought process, but it may be enough to affect your ability to make decisions during an emergency. The cold tends to raise the anxiety level and create additional stress. It not only slows your *mental* reaction to stimulus, but also slows your *physical* capability. Under stress and in times of emergency, this might mean a difference in safety. So, as a result, it is very important to protect the body in all water temperatures from any possible lowering of the core temperature. This is absolutely critical in colder water.

It is widely believed that the wet suit warms the body by allowing a thin layer of water to enter between the neoprene and the skin, which is then warmed and actually insulates the body. However, this is not altogether desirable, because if there is room for the water to enter in the first place, there is room for the water to circulate. If the water circulates, it must be continually rewarmed, which pulls body heat away. It is better to have a suit that fits so snugly that it stops all water circulation into, inside, or out of the suit. No water circulation lets you stay warmer than even very little circulation.

Wet Suit Material

Neoprene is available in several thicknesses. Thicker neoprene naturally provides more warmth. However, after a point there is a trade-off between the increased warmth and the increased effort required to move inside the stiffer, heavier material. Figure 2-3 indicates the amount of wet suit thickness you will probably need in water ranging in temperature from 35°F (5°C) to 75°F (24°C). Before selecting a suit, you should consider the type of diving you plan to do. If you are quite active, a slightly lighter suit might be more desirable because it gives you more flexibility and less resistance. On the other hand, if you are not very active underwater, you should wear thicker neoprene because it increases the insulation and the resistance of the material is not a significant factor.

Wet suits are constructed three different ways, as shown in figure 2-4. You can choose from suits which are unlined (skin-two side), lined with nylon on

WET SUIT THICKNESS	WATER TEMPERATURE
3/8 inch or dry suit	35°-50°F (1°-10°C)
3/8 or 1/4 inch	50°-60°F (10°-16°C)
1/4 or 3/16 inch	60°-70°F (16°-21°C)
3/16 or partial 1/4 inch	70°-75°F (21°24°C)
1/8 or partial 3/16 inch	75°F and above (24°C and above)

Fig. 2-3 Guide to Wet Suit Thickness

one side (nylon-one side), or lined with nylon on both sides (nylon-two side). Nylon is most generally used for lining, however, manufacturers have been testing many fabrics to determine their warmth, comfort, and durability.

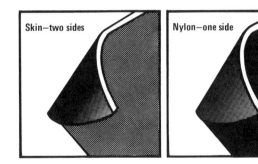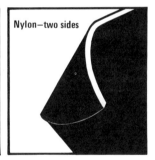

Fig. 2-4 Wet Suit Construction

There are advantages and disadvantages of having material adhered to the neoprene. Skin-two side has the most flexibility. It can also be cut tighter to the body which decreases the circulation of water and keeps you warmer than nylon-one or nylon-two. The disadvantages are that the neoprene alone is not very strong and the seams are bonded with glue, which does not hold the seams together adequately. Bare neoprene also tears quite easily and the nature of the material makes it difficult to put on and take off.

Having nylon on one side of the neoprene is better for wear and durability because the seams can be sewn on one side, which gives it more strength. Having nylon on the inside makes it easier to don and doff the suit, however, it still permits snagging and tearing on the outside. If the suit is lined only on the outside, the tearing and snagging problem is reduced, but the problem of getting into and out of the suit returns.

Suits with nylon on two sides eliminate most of the problems. This type of suit is easier to put on, is more durable, does not snag, and has stronger seams than the other two types of material. The disadvantages of having nylon on both sides are added stiffness, which increases somewhat with age, and reduced flexibility. Because of this, the suit cannot be cut as snug as the skin-two side and therefore is not quite so effective in reducing circulation, but the difference in flexibility and warmth between the two is minimal.

Wet Suit Selection

The critical areas of protection are the groin, under the arms, up the small of the back, along the sides, the head, and the neck. Two things determine how much protection a wet suit provides: general fit and the amount of material or insulation in these critical areas.

Excellent fit is the most important feature of the wet suit. A 3/16-inch suit that fits well is warmer than a thicker and heavier suit that does not fit. For most divers, a custom-made suit is best. For a suit to fit correctly, it should feel like a second skin; snug everywhere; not so tight as to restrict motion, but certainly tight enough to avoid circulation of water. (See figure 2-5.) The wet suit is warmer when the amount of water circulation is restricted.

Fig. 2-5 Perfect Wet Suit Fit

The hood and boots should be snug but not too tight. It is important that the hood opening around the face be small enough to allow a proper seal with the mask, as shown in figure 2-6. To fit correctly, the gloves should be tight enough to prevent water circulation but loose enough not to cause cramping.

The critical areas of protection in warm water above 80°F (27°C) are the groin, under the arms, and along the sides. The minimum amount of wet suit that can protect the torso is a vest, as shown in figure 2-7. However, that is all it protects. The shorty is much more desirable because it protects the groin, the sides, under the arms, and to a certain extent, the

Fig. 2-6 Proper Hood Fit

Fig. 2-7 Wet Suit Vest

Fig. 2-8 Shorty Wet Suit

neck and back. (See figure 2-8.) The only unprotected areas are the head, arms, and legs. This suit is generally satisfactory in water above 80°F (27°C). Another consideration for warm water is a very light, full suit which covers all the body except the head, feet, and hands, and which protects you from both temperature and accidental cuts and scrapes.

The areas of the body that need to be protected in water above 72°F (22°C) up to 80°F (27°C) are essentially the same as in warm water. However, it is important that the extremities be protected to prevent early shivering and resulting discomfort. The best suits for these temperatures are a one-piece jump suit, a standard two-piece suit, or a Farmer John, as shown in figure 2-9. The Farmer John adds a double layer of protection in the torso area. Of course, you can always wear a vest, but that should not be necessary in waters as warm as 72°F (22°C).

When you dive in cold water from 50°F (10°C) up to 70°F (21°C), you need to protect your body as thoroughly as possible. The body cools very rapidly and requires a full suit along with hood, boots, and gloves in 50°F (10°C) water. It becomes critical to protect the head,

Fig. 2-9 Farmer John

Fig. 2-10 Protection for Cold Water

neck, hands, and feet. An adequate suit for this type of water is a jump suit with a vest and possibly a neoprene swim suit, as shown in figure 2-10, or a standard two-piece suit with a vest, including hood, boots, and gloves. You can use other options, such as a vest with an attached hood or a jacket with an attached hood. The Farmer John wet suit worn with the vest and the neoprene swim suit offers maximum wet suit protection.

For very cold water below 50°F (10°C), you need all the protection that is available. The Farmer John pants provide one layer of protection over the torso. Then, you can wear a hooded vest and a jacket to give you three layers of material protecting the vital areas. A neoprene swim suit protects the groin and adds significantly to the comfort of the dive. If you plan to dive at these temperatures, you should definitely consider the advantages of a dry suit for the additional protection it provides.

MAINTENANCE

Problems with wet suits occur most often at the seams. Nylon-one side suits have seams sewn on at least one side. If the suit is a nylon-two side style, the seams are sewn on both sides. This double stitching greatly reduces the chances of seam separation. Some manufacturers also place tape on the seam lines. It is good to seal the loose ends of each seam with wet suit cement, as shown in figure 2-11. Tears are also easily repaired with wet suit cement. The correct way to apply the cement is to spread one light but thorough coat on both surfaces and allow it to dry until it is no longer tacky. Then apply a second coat and let it dry until it too is not tacky. Finally, join the surfaces and press them together to form a proper seal.

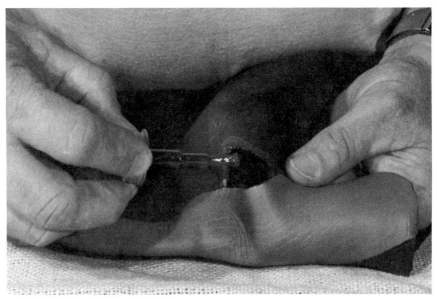

Fig. 2-11 Seams Sealed with Wet Suit Cement

Wet suits receive the most wear on the knees, elbows, and seat. This can be slowed or eliminated a great deal by adding pads to all these areas. Since they are on their knees frequently, photographers and shore divers find knee pads useful. The greatest wear to boots occurs along the sides of the soles. This can be reduced by using some of the better sole material. To slow wear on the sides, add extra material, as shown in figure 2-12. Because of the nature of glove use, it is almost impossible to prevent wear and they will be frequently replaced.

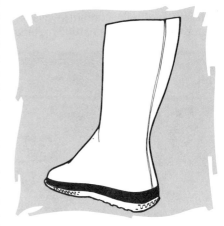

Fig. 2-12 Boot Modification

There are several other wet suit modifications you might consider. One is to add a spine pad. It is designed to keep cold water from flowing down your back by filling in the indentation along the spine. (See figure 2-13.) A pocket glued to the wet suit thigh is a good place to keep your knife. (See figure 2-14.) The pocket keeps the knife from moving around your leg or becoming entangled. Another handy pouch attached to the calf of your wet suit pants can hold extra tools and accessories.

The metal swivel fasteners or twist locks on the jacket's beavertail are prone to corrosion and breakage. You may want to replace them with velcro

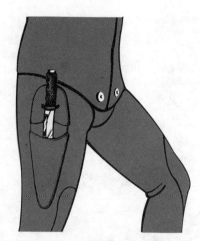

Fig. 2-13 Spine Pad   Fig. 2-14 Wet Suit Pocket

fasteners if they break, as shown in figure 2-15. Otherwise, thoroughly rinse the metal locks after each dive. Zippers, as well as the locks, should be lubricated with silicone. If you do not have silicone, use stick lubricant, soap, or candle wax to keep them from jamming.

If you want to get the most wear out of your wet suit, consider using coveralls. They are used to cover the dry suits of commercial divers, but protect wet suits as well. Check the fabric content and get the highest possible synthetic content available, because this wears longer and is less water absorbant than natural materials.

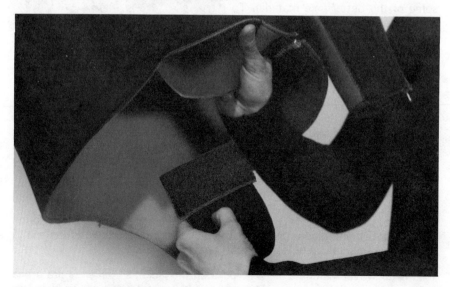

Fig. 2-15 Velcro Fasteners on Beavertail

DRY SUIT PROTECTION

The concept of the dry suit, as illustrated in figure 2-16, is that it provides complete protection from any exposure to the water and uses both air and cloth as insulators. As you add air inside the suit through the oral inflator, you create an increasingly larger barrier between the water and your skin. Once the air is warmed, heat does not leave your body as quickly as in a wet suit. You may experience the sensation of cold against your legs when you are upright in the water. When you lift your legs, the warm air surrounds the legs and an instant warming takes place.

Neoprene material is used for dry suits as well as for wet suits. The seams are sewn and sealed to prevent water from passing through them and waterproof zippers are installed, which completely seals the suit and creates an air environment between the skin and the neoprene. They can be used with or without clothing to act as an insulator between the skin and neoprene.

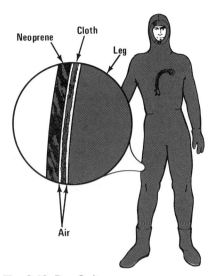

Fig. 2-16 Dry Suit

The dry suit really is considerably warmer than the wet suit. They do, however, have some disadvantages because they are bulky and tend to restrict mobility to a certain extent. They are not as flexible as wet suits. The increased amount of neoprene and trapped air requires that you add more weight to offset the increased buoyancy. This increased bulk and weight can cause you to tire more easily.

There are several different dry suits available, as shown in figure 2-17. They fall into two categories. Full dry suits completely keep water from reaching your body, with the possible exception of the hands and head. Partial dry suits protect just the arms, legs, and torso, but water does contact the feet, hands, and head. The full dry suit is warmer than the partial dry suit because it protects the entire body. The extremities thereby retain heat better than the partial dry suit.

As technology moves along, manufacturers experiment with more materials and designs for wet and dry suits as well as new devices to increase diver comfort. One day, this technology may provide maximum protection and flexibility with minimum restrictions. Remember to protect the core temperature and do not be fooled when the water "seems" to be warm. You must do what is necessary to provide yourself the kind of personal comfort that makes diving a pleasant and relaxing experience.

Fig. 2-17 Types of Dry Suits

COMMUNICATION

Attempting to communicate underwater has long been one of the most frustrating aspects of scuba diving, because you are emersed in an environment with so many beautiful things to see and experiences to share, but without special devices or hand signals, you have no feasible means to convey to your buddy what you are experiencing. There are three basic ways to communicate underwater: by hand signals, by simple mechanical devices that are a part of the equipment worn by most divers and by electronic communicators.

HAND SIGNALS

Several hand signals, in addition to the basic safety signals, are used commonly to communicate underwater. They make it possible to convey messages on a higher level than using basic signals alone. Many signals are particular to a local region or they may be ones you and your buddy have personally devised. (See figure 2-18.) It is also useful to learn parts of the manual alphabet and certain signals used in manual communication if you desire a more precise means of communicating with your hands or if you or your buddy has a hearing loss. (See figure 2-19 and 2-20.) But these still do not give you the full opportunity to share your experiences and their excitement as they happen.

Fig. 2-18 Hand Signals

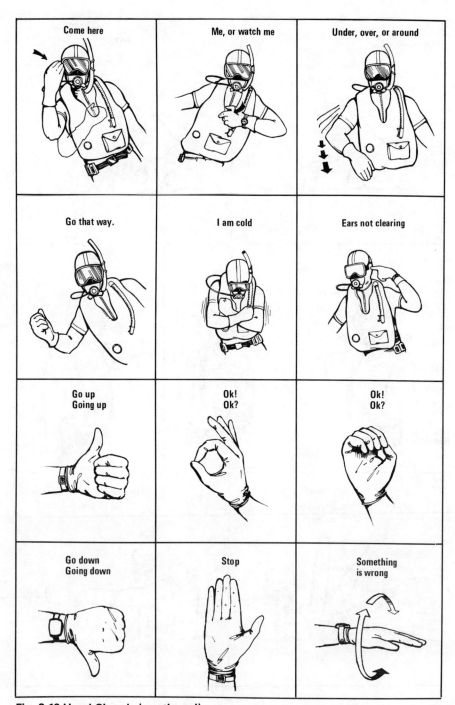

Fig. 2-18 Hand Signals (continued)

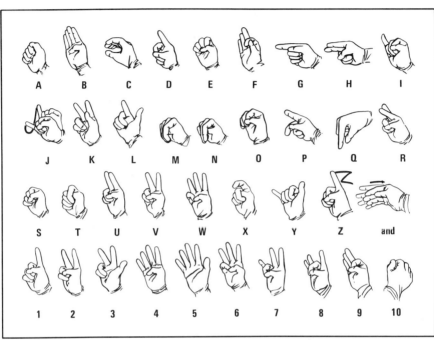

Fig. 2-19 Manual Alphabet (The National Association of the Deaf)

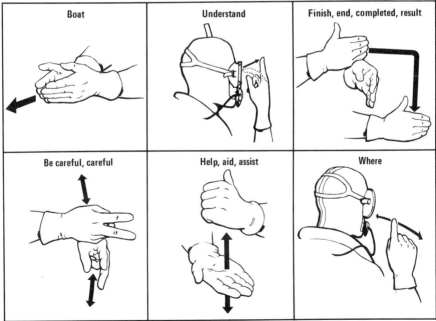

Fig. 2-20 Manual Communication (The National Association of the Deaf) For a book on the complete language of manual communication, contact your local Deaf Center.

SIMPLE COMMUNICATION METHODS

While it is almost impossible for sound to be transmitted from air into the heavier density of water, you can do it to a certain extent. You can transmit some sound to your buddy by shouting very loudly, but you must be close together. Even then, you can usually decipher little of what is being conveyed. It is also possible to speak through the standard scuba regulator, but it is almost impossible to make yourself understood, partly because the mouthpiece jumbles your speech, and also because the area of the mouthpiece and second stage does not provide sufficient resonance to develop and transmit sound into the water.

An alternative is a commercially-manufactured unit which creates an artificial air pocket and has good resonating material. This method of communication works, but it is not outstanding because it requires that you take a breath of air, use that air to speak, place the regulator back into your mouth, and take another breath before you can speak again. This is undesirable and potentially hazardous. It is not suitable for normal underwater communication.

ELECTRONIC COMMUNICATORS

Three basic styles of electronic communicators are available, but only two are suitable for sport diving. One is geared more to light commercial work, and although you could use it, this communicator is impractical for sport diving.

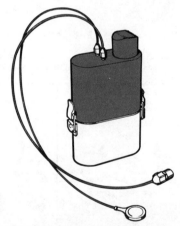

Some communicators utilize either a throat microphone or the same microphone placed inside the mouth. (See figure 2-21.) These have two main disadvantages. The throat microphone relies strictly on vibration from the throat into the microphone, which does not give it the necessary quality for real clarity. Placing a microphone inside your mouth and trying to speak around it, particularly while you also have a regulator in your mouth, can create some rather severe but not insurmountable disadvantages with clarity.

Fig. 2-21 Electronic Communicators

Another electronic communicator, shown in figure 2-22, permits the microphone to be placed close to the mouth, and allows the lips to move

Fig.2-22 Electronic Communicator Use

freely. You are able to form the words more carefully, and the quality of transmission is significantly improved. This system is the most desirable of the two currently available for sport diving.

HELMET COMMUNICATION

The helmet, as shown in figure 2-23, creates an air atmosphere around the head. This improves underwater communication in two ways. First, the type of microphone used is superior and since you speak into an air atmosphere, the resonance and word formations are vastly improved.

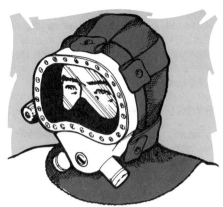

Fig. 2-23 Helmet Communication

The ability to hear is also improved because the sound is transmitted into the air instead of water. The primary problems with this system are its expense, it usually requires a wire connected to the surface, and it requires more sophisticated training than used in normal sport diver training.

The basic problem of underwater communication has plagued divers and manufacturers for many years. They are constantly working on improving the quality of the mechanical components as well as standard techniques of underwater communication. There are many possibilities for the future that look promising.

EXTENDED DIVES

One continuing desire of sport divers is to stay down longer. There has been a constant search since the original development of scuba to give the diver longer bottom times, however there are few available options.

One approach to this problem is larger tanks, which simply provide more capacity, but this is generally impractical because larger tanks mean increased weight and reduced mobility. A second solution is multiple tanks and a third option is higher pressure. The standard 71.2 cubic foot tank is normally rated for 2,250 psi and provides about an hour of down time for the average diver in less than 33 feet of water. Other tanks normally used are the 3,000 psi models available in the 70, 80, and 100 cubic foot sizes. The 80 and 100 sizes provide another 20 to 30 minutes of bottom time. While this may not be a significant increase, it is an improvement over the smaller capacity tanks.

Some tanks can hold up to 4,500 psi, which effectively doubles the capacity of a tank the size of the 71.2. However, the additional steel needed for these tanks to hold the increased pressure greatly increases the weight therefore decreasing mobility. The safety of the tanks is also decreased somewhat because of the reduced buoyancy.

The 4,500-psi tank or any pressures approaching 4,500 psi are somewhat impractical because most air refill stations lack the capacity to fill to that high pressure level. Improvements in available tank metals and the development of experimental cylinders using such things as layered material or wire wrapping may eventually decrease tank weight while increasing tank pressure capacities.

CRYOGENIC SCUBA

Cryogenic scuba has been experimented with for many years and is not a new concept. Cryogenic scuba uses liquid oxygen and nitrogen which are much more concentrated than compressed gases. It utilizes a system, like that shown in figure 2-24, in which the liquid is stored separately in two thermos-like bottles. As both elements come out of their liquid state and are formed into gas, they are mixed in correct proportion to form a breathing mixture.

It is conceivable that this may be a possible way to extend bottom times for the future, but much like higher pressure tanks, it creates two problems. One problem with cryogenic scuba is that liquid nitrogen and oxygen are not readily available and the other problem is that for oxygen and nitrogen to remain in a liquid state, they must be kept at very low temperature. Therefore, it is not practical to store it for long periods in tanks. The tanks must be filled almost immediately before the actual dive. Many refinements must be made, not only in the equipment itself, but also in production of the breathing elements and storage capabilities before the cryogenic unit can reach the level of practicality needed for sport diving.

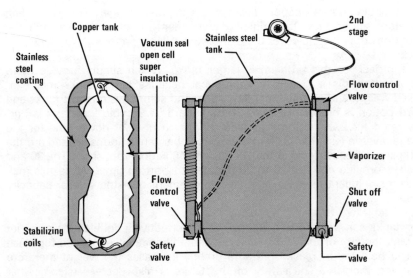

Fig. 2-24 Cryogenic Scuba

SURFACE-SUPPLIED AIR

While surface-supplied air is not generally considered to be part of scuba diving because you depend on the surface supply to breathe, it is possible to use scuba and surface-supplied air interchangably during a single dive. The hooka unit, shown in figure 2-25, is a combination of surface-supplied air and the scuba regulator. It functions on the same demand principle as the scuba regulator. The surface compressor pumps into a storage unit which functions much like a scuba cylinder, but with a virtually inexhaustible air supply. The storage unit is a high-capacity

Fig. 2-25 Surface-Supplied Air

system that remains on the surface. A hose connects the storage unit to the first stage of the regulator. Another hooka-type unit works directly off the compressor with a constant flow of air into the mask or mouthpiece.

The main drawbacks of these systems are they limit your mobility and diving range and they are not acceptable for general sightseeing underwater. Their best application is for light commercial or scientific work which may require you to remain in a small area for long time periods. For the present, or until dramatic scientific breakthroughs occur which might permit actually removing air from the ambient water, sport divers are confined to the available self-contained sources of air.

ADDITIONAL EQUIPMENT

In addition to items needed for safer, more comfortable, and longer diving, there is equipment which permits you to advance into other areas of interest beyond simply using scuba gear. Propulsion units, underwater metal detectors, and hand-held sonar increase mobility, add significantly to hobbies, or, in some cases, permit safe return to the entry/exit point. Two other pieces of equipment, a dive computer and a regulator that is part of the manual inflation device, indicate the latest developments in diving equipment. While there are other items available, these pieces of equipment draw the most practical interest.

PROPULSION UNITS

The propulsion units, as shown in figure 2-26, increase your mobility underwater and add to the enjoyment of a dive. They are motor-driven and use battery power to move at speeds from one to three knots, which is about as fast as you can move comfortably without too much drag on the body. Even if you turn your head while moving at this speed, the resistance of the water can remove your mask.

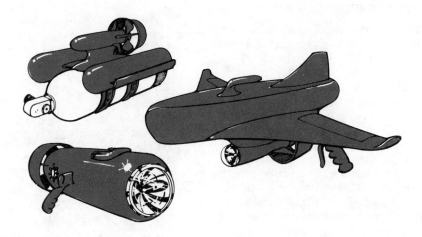

Fig. 2-26 Propulsion Unit

These units have variable range and power capabilities. Some units with two motors have the capabilities of pulling more than one diver at sustained speeds of one to three knots. Depending on the battery's size and durability and whether the unit is used continuously or intermittently, propulsion units can run from one to four hours.

METAL DETECTORS

Several metal detectors are available and depending on where they are used, they may detect anything from steel to gold. They can pick up signals from 6 to 12 inches beneath the bottom, as shown in figure 2-27. Metal detectors work very much like sonar — they send out a pulse that reflects off metal objects. The returning pulse triggers an audible impulse in the metal detector,

Fig. 2-27 Metal Detector Use

so you can tell when you have "hit" metal. An increased impulse activity indicates not only the location but the magnitude of the object. Metal detectors can add significantly to the interest of diving, as well as helping you locate lost objects and such things as underwater cables or pipelines. These units are relatively inexpensive and can add significantly to the potential joy of diving.

HAND-HELD SONAR

In terms of safety and the capability of returning to or moving toward a predetermined spot, hand-held sonar is a significant improvement over the compass. In this type of sonar, a transponder hangs from the boat or at the entry/exit point, as shown in figure 2-28. A hand-held transducer picks up the signals transmitted by the transponder and indicates by increased sound activity that whoever is holding it is moving in the correct direction.

Fig. 2-28 Hand-Held Sonar

DIVE COMPUTER

A dive computer, as shown in figure 2-29, is being devised to give the diver several types of information from one compact unit. The digital readouts on this computer indicate dive time, surface interval times, depth, required

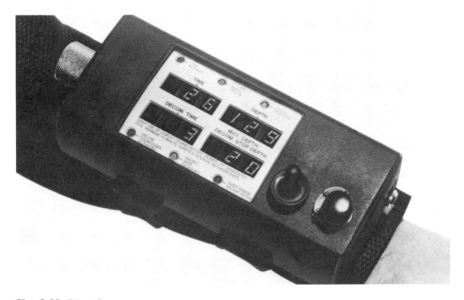

Fig. 2-29 Dive Computer

decompression time, maximum depth, and required depth of decompression stops. Various lights are activated if decompression becomes necessary, to warn the diver five minutes before decompression is necessary, for decompression countdown, to warn the diver of ascent over 60 feet per minute, to warn if the diver exceeds the maximum operating limit, and to show low battery function.

ALTERNATE INFLATION REGULATOR

The alternate inflation regulator combines the functions of the infla-

Fig. 2-30 Alternate Inflation Regulator

tion/deflation device on the buoyancy control device and the octopus regulator. (See figure 2-30.) It can be installed on the buoyancy control device and is inflated or deflated by depressing the appropriate button.

The demand regulator is for emergency breathing only and is not to be used in place of the primary breathing regulator. It can supplement or replace the octopus regulator and can be connected to the main tank or a separate "pony bottle." To use this regulator in a buddy breathing situation, you would give your primary regulator to your buddy and use the alternate inflation regulator yourself. This device can be used with a reserve air supply. In both situations, you must have sufficient air capacity, especially at depth.

As sport diving grows, many such specialty items will be developed to enhance the enjoyment of the sport and to provide additional safety measures. At the present, however, it is enough to have a good understanding of why protection from the cold is so important to your personal comfort, how to add to your safety and enjoyment by monitoring vital information, and how to communicate with your buddy so you might be safer and able to share your experiences on a moment-to-moment basis. Hopefully, at some point in the future, you may be able to stay down longer to further study or simply enjoy the beauty of the underwater environment. Understanding these things adds to the overall enjoyment and safety of the sport and are important to today's sport diver.

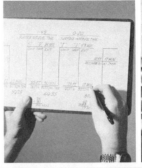

PART III
boat diving

Introduction

Diving from boats has been part of sport diving from the very beginning of the sport. Now it is the fastest growing diving activity. Charter or commercial dive boats are used in diving areas where no boats were previously found. More boats operate in established boat diving areas and these are becoming larger and better equipped, with many built strictly for diving. At the same time, more divers use private boats.

Divers now ask for more and better services; and diving instruction, techniques, and equipment have improved to where it is worthwhile to build and operate large, commercial, dive boats. These improved boats give sport divers a taste of the ease and fun of boat diving and, in turn, stimulate the increased use of both private and commercial small dive boats.

dive boats, commercial boat diving, boating for the owner/operator

The dive boat provides a base of operations where you can rest, change gear, eat, get warm, and talk. (See figure 3-1.) This contributes to the safety, security, ease, comfort, and the very joy of diving. Boat diving lets you dive in areas where it would not otherwise be possible and, at the same time, lets you enjoy diving activities not possible from shore.

In some areas, boats are often the only way to dive in water that is calm, clear, or deep. It is best to do night diving from a boat. Hunting, collecting, wreck diving, underwater photography, search and recovery, light salvage, and drift diving are all best done from a boat. Boats also provide a social

Fig. 3-1 Dive Boat

Fig. 3-2 Social Aspects of Boat Diving

aspect to diving — an opportunity to interact with fellow divers who share this common interest, as shown in figure 3-2.

Yet, with all that boat diving has to offer, there are still possible difficulties. You may have had no preparation for boat diving during your training. You may have been on small, uncomfortable boats. You may not know how to find a dive boat or how to act when on board. You may be concerned about getting seasick. All these are reasonable concerns because they interfere with safe, comfortable, and enjoyable diving.

This material provides information about the characteristics of dive boats, how to find a dive boat, how to prepare for a boat dive, making your boat diving more enjoyable, specific boat diving techniques, and how to operate diving activities from your own boat.

DIVE BOATS

TYPES

Charter or commercial dive boats are businesses that provide diving trips. These boats vary greatly in size, arrangement, and equipment, but are very similar to sport fishing boats. The first dive boats were converted from sport fishing or military boats. Now boats are often built specifically for diving, but the hull and superstructure still resemble fishing boats. (See figure 3-3.) In some areas where less boat diving is done, boats may alternate between carrying divers and fishermen.

Fig. 3-3 Converted Dive Boat

Private boats used for diving may be any type or size. Large luxury yachts, cabin cruisers, sailboats, open outboards, and inflatable boats are all used. Small open boats with outboard motors, including both inflatables, as shown in figure 3-4, and hard materials, such as wood, metal, and fiberglass, have become the most popular private boats for diving. Inflatable boats are easy to transport and can be used almost anywhere. Small boats are less expensive, easier to maneuver and dive from, and most often faster than large boats. They usually need very few modifications for diving.

Fig. 3-4 Inflatable Dive Boat

Another category of surface support includes surface floats, such as inner tubes, surf mats, paddleboards, surfboards, kayaks, and so forth. (See figure 3-5.) These floats are valuable safety tools for divers. They are not actually *boats*, but they do provide some of the same advantages, such as a place to rest, store extra gear or game, adjust gear, discuss the dive, and make rescues. These surface floats are most often used on dives made from shore, but they also may be used from boats. Using floats may help to keep from moving the boat or they may be used to increase your range of activities.

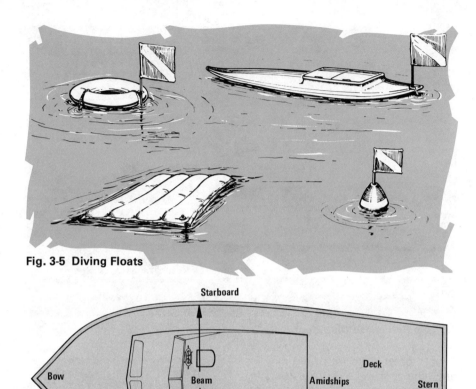

Fig. 3-5 Diving Floats

Starboard

Bow

Beam

Deck

Amidships

Stern

Port

Fig. 3-6 Top View of Boat

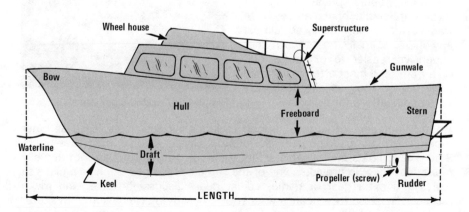

Wheel house

Superstructure

Bow

Gunwale

Hull

Freeboard

Stern

Waterline

Draft

Keel

Propeller (screw)

Rudder

LENGTH

Fig. 3-7 Side View of Boat

PARTS OF A BOAT

You will naturally be more comfortable on a boat if you know the names and appearance of different parts and equipment. Figures 3-6 and 3-7 show the general parts of a boat; figure 3-8 indicates the general layout for a dive boat.

When you face the *bow*, you are said to be facing *forward*. Turning around and facing the *stern*, you are looking *aft*. The *bilge* is the lower inside area of the *hull*. *Bulkheads* are the walls, *decks* refer to the floor, *ladders* are steps, and *overhead* is the ceiling. The *galley* is the kitchen and the *head* is the bathroom.

An *anchor* is a specially-shaped metal device designed to dig into the bottom underwater and hold the boat in place. A *mooring* is a semi-permanent anchorage with a heavy anchor, chain, buoy, and line.

A *fathom* is a measure of length used on boats and in the water. It is equal to six feet. The direction away from the wind is called *leeward*, and *windward* means facing into the wind. The sideways rotational motion of a boat is called *roll*, while the vertical rise and fall of the bow is called *pitching*. *Yaw* is when the bow falls off course to either side.

COMMERCIAL BOAT DIVING

Most diving is done from commercial dive boats. You may choose to dive from a small or large commercial dive boat. There are several things to consider before selecting the type of boat from which you want to dive. These include licensing of both the boat and operator, what type of equipment is available, activities offered in the area the boat is going, and other

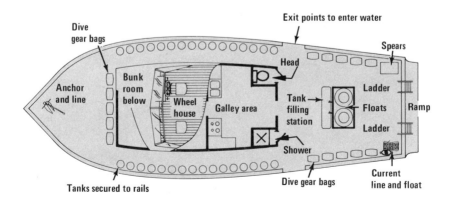

Fig. 3-8 Top View of Dive Boat

aspects. Make sure any boat you choose is properly set up for diving, otherwise, it could be difficult to dive from.

COAST GUARD REQUIREMENTS

When diving in or off the shores of the United States, you should not go on a boat diving trip unless certain U.S. Coast Guard requirements are met. These requirements are your assurance that the boat is safe, has proper equipment, and the operator is qualified. Most foreign countries have no requirements, so, when boat diving in foreign waters, you should do your own thorough safety check.

U.S. Coast Guard requirements create two distinct categories of boats. Large boats that carry more than six passengers for hire are required to have both the boat and operator licensed by the Coast Guard. A passenger for hire is any person who has contributed anything directly or indirectly for the passage. This could be money, food, gas, and so forth. Any operator should be knowledgeable about boats and navigation and on larger boats, have someone to help. Smaller dive boats that carry six or less passengers for hire, as shown in figure 3-9, are required to only have the operator licensed, however, the boat is still required to meet certain Coast Guard requirements. If the boat license and operator license, as shown in figure 3-10, are prominently displayed, you can feel more at ease and do less careful checking.

Fig. 3-9 Small Dive Boat

Fig. 3-10 Operator License

EQUIPMENT

Several items of equipment are required. There should be more personal flotation devices (PFD's) than people on the boat. Larger boats need to have a float or raft. Other equipment should include anchors, lines, compass, first aid kit, radio, and oxygen resuscitator or inhalator. Portable fire extinguishers are required on all boats. These are the relatively obvious and vital things that should be provided.

The dive boat should have additional equipment, such as a current line measuring 100 to 300 feet with float, extra floats, dive flags, and a recall system. The Sport Diver flag, shown in figure 3-11, is used throughout North America. The International Code of Signals flag, also shown, means "I have a diver down, keep well clear at slow speed."

Fig. 3-11 Diving Flags

An electronic underwater recall system is used by diving boats. This system sends a warning sound similar to a police siren into the water. The recall system is used when the boat's anchor is dragging, the weather has deteriorated, a diver has had an accident, or some other emergency action is needed. If you ever hear such a siren, surface as soon as it is safe to do so and look toward the boat for the crews' signal either to come to the boat or remain where you are.

As boat diving has grown, dive boats have become larger, faster, and more comfortable. Boats used in each diving area vary in equipment and arrangement. This is based on weather and diving conditions, length of boat runs to dive sites, length of time divers spend on the boat, plus the variety of diving activities done in the area. Some improvements becoming more common include:

1. One or more high pressure compressors on board
2. Large boarding ramps or platforms and ladders
3. Showers, often with hot water
4. Bunk rooms
5. Galley for food
6. Electronic navigation equipment, including radar fathometer, and loran
7. Special dive gear racks

Smaller boats used for shorter trips usually have no room for these items, nor would you need to have them. The smaller dive boats have short runs, usually taking less than an hour to reach a dive site. They usually make only one dive per trip with a total trip time averaging between two and four hours.

SELECTING A COMMERCIAL DIVE BOAT

Once you have an idea of what commercial dive boats look like, how they are equipped, and what you should look for, you will want to actually find a good dive boat. These boats are often chartered by diving businesses or groups. Other times, individual tickets are sold directly. There are several places to find specific information on dive boat trips.

1. Local dive stores
2. Local dive clubs
3. Diving magazines and newsletters
4. Local commercial boat landings
5. National underwater instructor associations
6. Travel agents who specialize in diving trips
7. The yellow pages in harbor areas under "Boats, Charter"

Each of these sources can help you with local boat trips or they may suggest special trips in a diving resort area. Other divers are also good sources of information. Figure 3-12 shows a checklist of questions you need to ask about each dive boat and dive boat trip you are considering.

DATE OF TRIP: _____

TIME OF DEPARTURE: _____RETURN: _____

DESTINATION (DIVE SITES): _____

BOAT NAME: _____ DOCK LOCATION: _____

DIRECTIONS: _____

_____

_____

DIVING DIFFICULTY: _____

DIVING ACTIVITIES: _____

COMPRESSOR ON BOAT? _____ BRING EXTRA TANKS? _____

GALLEY ON BOAT? _____BRING OWN FOOD? _____

ANY REQUIRED SLEEPING GEAR? _____

SPECIAL LOCAL INFORMATION: _____

IF PRINTED INFORMATION AVAILABLE, TAKE COPY: _____

Fig. 3-12 Boat Trip Checklist

You may pay for the trip directly to the boat or through the dive store, landing, club, or travel agent. Be sure to take your receipt and/or ticket along with some extra money when you go on a trip.

DIVE PREPARATION

You will definitely want to prepare for your trip as thoroughly as possible to insure a safe and enjoyable boat dive. The first idea is to plan and prepare everything with your regular dive buddy, if possible. You can meet divers on the boat and become buddies for the day, but it is far better to share the entire dive experience with someone you know.

Training and Experience

Unless you learned to dive in an area where boat diving is common, you probably did not receive training for this activity. Some advanced diving courses offer boat diving instruction, if not, ask your instructor to include it in the course.

Diving experience increases your ability to relax and your physical fitness. It maintains skills and teaches you to handle many situations in the water. Diving from shore not only makes you appreciate boat diving more, but also prepares you for this activity. Be sure to select boat diving trips that are within your capability.

Equipment

Your equipment needs to be in the best possible condition and ready for your boat diving trip. After all the time of preparation and finally reaching the dive site, plus the cost of the trip, you would not want a piece of equipment to ruin your day of diving. So, pack an extra mask strap, fin strap, "O" rings, snorkel holder, dust cap, CO_2 cartridges, high pressure plug, wet suit cement, silicone, tape, and so forth. In some cases, the boat crew may have some of these parts, but you cannot rely on this and, in some cases, their parts may not fit your gear.

Several days before the trip, check all your equipment. This gives you time to replace parts, make repairs, and rent replacement gear if something of yours needs to be repaired. Inflate the buoyancy control system, breathe from the regulator, check the tank pressure, and carefully go over your wet suit and apply glue as needed. Check CO_2 cartridges, all straps, and so on.

You should have your tank filled, even if the boat has a compressor. Boat compressors are often slower and have lower pressure than shore-based compressors and may charge more per fill. By having your tank full, you are ready for the first dive and if the boat compressor breaks down, you can still make this dive.

Your dive gear should be stored as neatly, securely, and compactly as possible. The tank and weight belt should be kept separate. You either carry them or wear them while you are loading the boat. One large gear bag for the gear that gets wet and one smaller bag for dry things is a good arrangement. (See figure 3-13.) These bags can be either the carry-on or the backpack type.

Fig. 3-13 Gear Bags for Boat Diving

You will want to pack your gear so the mask, regulator, decompression meter, and other delicate items are separate from each other and are protected by wet suit parts or other soft gear. Before loading your gear bag and after checking each item for proper function, go through the gear in the order you put it on, to make sure you have it all. A list of your equipment is a great help. Then pack it into the gear bag in reverse order, such as, fins in first and wet suit pants in near the last so you can put on your gear as you remove it from the bag.

Fitness
You will want to be generally fit for diving. This includes adequate rest, a well-balanced diet, and regular exercise. Because dive boats often leave during the night or very early in the morning, your sleeping schedule may be disturbed. In addition, you will probably dive more often and deeper than usual on a boat trip, requiring you to expend more energy. Therefore, it is important to get as much rest as possible the day or two before the dive and sleep on the boat if possible during the trip to and from the dive site.

The two meals before the boat trip and any food eaten on the boat should be light and nourishing — food you can easily digest. For at least 12 hours before the trip, you should not drink any alcohol or use any drugs.

The increased amount of diving done on boats makes it necessary to be able to clear your ears easily. By equalizing the pressure in your ears during the 24 hours before the dive, while on the boat, and at the surface, it is far easier to clear them as you descend. If you have difficulty equalizing, you may wish to take some medication. Take only medication you have safely taken before. Bring some of the medication on the trip in case it wears off, do not use medication to mask symptoms which would normally prevent you from diving, and always check with your doctor. These guidelines apply to any other prescription or nonprescription drugs you may need to take.

Dive Planning
Both you and your buddy should contribute to all dive planning. Above all, you each reserve the right to make the "no-dive" decision, based on changing medical, physical, psychological, or environmental conditions. If something is wrong, do not dive just because you traveled a great distance and paid your money.

Boat diving increases the range of possible diving activities, improves your ability to deal with diving conditions, and makes it possible to come back and regroup if you or your buddy have a problem. Using the dive boat as a surface support station makes the planning and the diving much easier.

BOAT DIVING TECHNIQUES
General Conduct
Boat diving, more than any other diving activity, brings people into close contact and your behavior affects other divers, just as their behavior affects

you. Divers tend to be an independent, self-sufficient group of people. This can be balanced and enhanced by the interpersonal relations possible on a dive boat. Each diver should be capable, well-trained, experienced, physically fit, and well-equipped. Still, you can place some reliance on and expect some help from your buddy, other divers, and the boat crew. They, in turn, should be able to expect this from you.

A day of boat diving can be enjoyable and safe if you have a positive attitude and you meet some personal responsibilities. First, look forward to the boat trip, and prepare yourself and your gear. Arrive early, about one-half hour or more before the trip. Ask where you should put your gear and stow it out of the way.

Greet other people while making eye contact and start conversations. Relax and settle down for a pleasant day of diving. This is a good time to find a diving buddy if you do not have one. You will want to find a place to sleep or sit during the boat ride during this time.

Because dive boats are often crowded, it is both a courteous and safer gesture to help someone don a tank, adjust a strap, or adjust a buoyancy control device. You should keep your gear together as much as possible and work out of your gear bag. Your gear should be marked with your name, some tape, or paint, because it is very easy to mix dive gear on a boat. Marking gear also helps tell divers apart underwater.

Boat Procedures
Look around the boat to get an idea of where things are and get to know the boat as well as possible. Ask the crew or someone who has been on board previously if you need something or do not understand a procedure. The procedures and others have been devised by the boat crew to better serve you. Even if you have been on another dive boat, these procedures may not be obvious. Boats often require you to show your certification card and to put your name on a roll sheet and on your tank. Some boats supply the tanks and weight belts and many boats have special ways and places for storing gear. (See figure 3-14.)

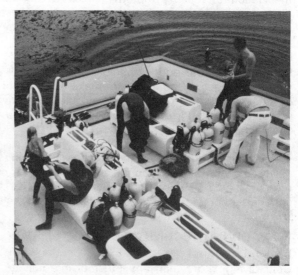

Fig. 3-14 Gear Storage on Dive Boat

Fig. 3-15 Dive Boat Galley

The marine toilet or *head* is sometimes quite different from a usual toilet. If instructions are not posted, be sure to ask. Put all trash in the trash can, not in the head, and do not throw any trash overboard. You should stay out of the boat's wheelhouse and engine room. Sometimes the crew may invite you to see the wheelhouse or if you have a special interest, you might ask to see it. Respect their wishes, as they have a responsibility to all passengers, the boat, and other vessels.

Between dives, relax, and take off as much gear as is practical. Most divers leave their wet suits on. Weight belts and tanks in particular should be taken off carefully and as soon as possible. Most boats do not allow dive gear or wet divers in the bunk room or galley. Some boats now allow divers in wet suits to use the galley between dives, as shown in figure 3-15, but all other gear should still be left outside. The crew can gather items you may need from your bunk. During this time, talk over the interesting sights and events of the dive while planning the next dive. This is also a good time to eat. Be sure to keep your dive gear and game together and out of the way.

Boats often move to another dive site between dives. This adds to the amount of time you have to relax and prepare for the next dive, as well as providing a surface interval for decompression. During this time, the crew fills tanks. Each boat has a different system for filling tanks. (See figure 3-16.) Some use tags, others have you place the tank in a certain location or remove the pack. Be sure to ask about the procedure.

At each new dive site, the crew will tell you the conditions, such as depth, current, special features, and procedures. If you are not clear on a certain point, be sure to ask. Before the boat moves, a visual and verbal roll call is taken. Be sure to only answer for yourself. Some dive boats have a divemaster who checks you in and out of the water for each dive.

When the crew is handling the anchor, as shown in figure 3-17, another smaller boat, or other heavy equipment, stand clear for your own safety. If a diving or boating emergency develops while you are on board, stay out of the crew's way and follow their instructions. Let the crew know if you have special skills, such as medical, mechanical, or instructional that may help.

If you plan to take any game, you need a fishing license and you need to know what is legal to take. Also be sure to have a container for your game. A burlap bag is best. Many dive boats now have their own additional rules on taking game, out of concern for the environment where the boat regularly takes divers. Check with the crew on any rules and respect them. Safety with spears is of prime importance. When you are not using your speargun, remove or cover the speargun and do all loading and unloading of spears away from the boat and other divers.

Motion Sickness

If you have a problem with motion sickness, it is a good idea to eat light, easily digestible foods, and take some medication before the trip. Many people feel better if they lie down and sleep. This is aided by many motion sickness medications that make people drowsy. The best place to sleep is down as low and as near the center line and middle of the boat as possible because this part of the boat moves the least. Also, stay away from engine, galley, or head fumes.

Other people can better handle motion sickness by staying on the deck in the fresh air. It is best to watch the horizon because this gives you a steady reference point. If you do vomit, go to the leeward side of the boat near the stern.

Preparing to Dive

Before the first dive, do not rush to get dressed. The skipper often takes time to carefully maneuver the boat right over the dive site. Be sure the skipper gives the "OK" before you get ready or enter the water.

As you put on your dive gear, help your buddy and let your buddy help you, as shown in figure 3-18. Hold the tank as your buddy puts it on and then reverse the process. Do not put a tank on over your head because there is the possibility of hitting someone, or falling if the boat moves. Never leave your

Fig. 3-16 Filling Tanks

Fig. 3-17 Crew Handling Anchor

tank standing unattended, because it could be knocked over very easily. Be careful to lean forward and step into your weight belt and not swing it around you. This avoids hitting some other diver. You should also avoid sitting on the deck when other divers are donning gear, since your head is right at the level of other divers' tank bottoms.

When you and your buddy are dressed, do a complete buddy gear check and review your dive plan away from the boat's exit point to avoid congestion. Put your fins on last near the exit point so you will not need to walk in them.

Fig. 3-18 Buddy Assistance

Depending on how the dive boat is arranged and the number of divers on board, you may need to jump into the water from some height. It is not always necessary to jump; you may be able to climb down a ladder or roll off the ramp or swim step. When you jump into the water, as shown in figure 3-19, you should use the following techniques:

1. Use the lowest exit point.
2. Put some air in your buoyancy control system.
3. Put the scuba regulator in your mouth.
4. Hold your octopus regulator on your weight belt buckle.
5. Watch how the boat swings and enter when it is away from your side.
6. Look to see that the water is clear.
7. Hold your mask.
8. Step down and out into the water, doing a gentle giant stride.

Once you are in the water, have any accessory gear, such as spearguns and cameras, handed down to you in the water. A line of 8 to 12 feet with a clip is good for this. Then, move away from the boat on the surface and look back and wait for your buddy. Before descending, do one more buddy check.

The Dive

One of the many advantages of boat diving is that you can often descend and ascend right by the boat, eliminating the need to snorkel. After your final buddy check on the surface, clear your ears, even though you have not yet started your descent. Go on scuba, deflate your buoyancy control device and exhale to start the descent. It is best to descend slowly and feet-first, while controlling your buoyancy, checking your instruments, clearing your ears, and keeping track of your buddy. You can use the anchor line for descending and ascending, but if the boat is rising and falling in a surge, keep the line at arm's length.

Fig. 3-19 Entry from Boat

Be aware of currents by observing seaweeds, bubbles, or your drift. If there is a current, dive into it so you can return with the current at the end of the dive. In areas of very strong currents, nearly all diving is done from boats. One method of *current diving* is to anchor the boat and dive in an area up-current from the boat. A line called the *lead line* is attached from the anchor line, directly to the stern of the boat. Another line with a float, called either a *current* or *trail line*, is trailed to the stern. (See figure 3-20.) You enter the

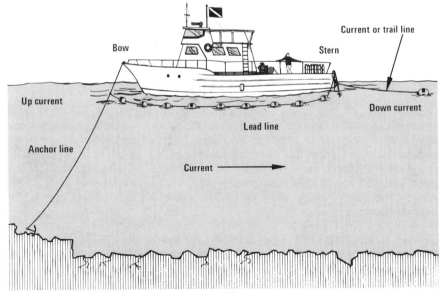

Fig. 3-20 Line Arrangement in Current Diving

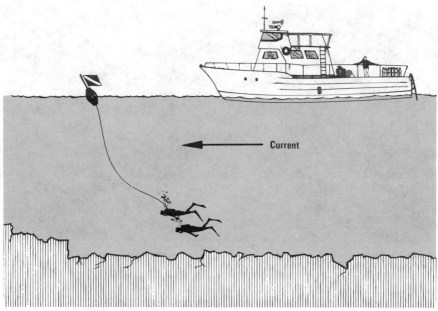

Fig. 3-21 Float Diving

water holding the lead line and pull yourself to the anchor line and then on down. You do not kick when you are on the line. At the bottom, you dive into the current and then return by the anchor line, to the lead line, then to the stern of the boat, and out of the water.

A *float dive* in a current is done with a float on the surface and line to the divers on the bottom, as shown in figure 3-21. As the divers move, the boat follows the float. At the end of the dive, the divers surface by the float and are picked up by the boat. *Drift diving* is done by lifting the boat's anchor off the bottom and letting the boat drift with the divers. You stay near or hold onto the anchor as you drift. (See figure 3-22.)

Another form of drift diving, often called *live boating*, is usually done from larger dive boats. In this case, the boat is underway, clear of divers, and does not have any anchor or floats in the water. You and your buddy get completely ready and enter the water as close together as possible. You should know the compass course of the drift so you later know where to look for the boat. You and your buddy make the dive drifting free with the current. At the end of the dive, surface very carefully — looking up, raising one hand, moving slowly, and listening.

On the surface, you and your buddy fully inflate your buoyancy control devices and join any other divers who are nearby. The boat usually starts down-current, picking up divers, so you are drifting toward the boat. (See figure 3-23.) Wait for the boat to come to you while you get ready. When the boat arrives, listen and watch for the crew's instructions. Be sure to do what

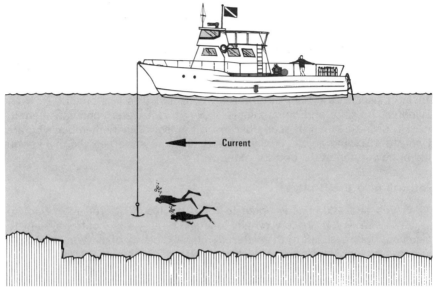

Fig. 3-22 Drift Diving

they say. When the boat stops, or you are given the "come on" signal, board as quickly as possible with all your gear in place.

When you dive in currents, just as in deep diving, wreck diving, and night diving, go with a diver who is experienced in this type of diving. Preferably, this would be an underwater instructor or guide.

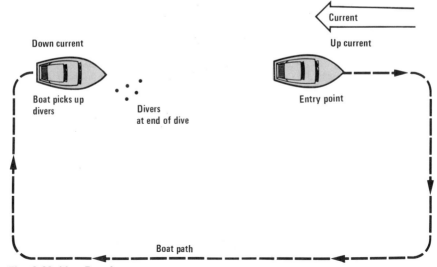

Fig. 3-23 Live Boating

If your dive is far from the boat's anchor, it is common practice to surface after you have used one-half to two-thirds of your air and check the boat's position, presuming your dive does not require decompression stops. Some divers like to do this several times during one dive.

Make each successive dive of the day easier by not diving as deep or as long, staying closer to the boat, and making your activities less strenuous. Your diving will be safer and more enjoyable this way. If water conditions permit, go skin diving instead of scuba diving on the last dive. Remember, you are diving to relax and enjoy yourself. This is far more important than what you find or how much of the bottom you cover.

Returning to the Boat

When you and your buddy agree to return to the boat, you may want to surface swim if you are low on air. Inflate the buoyancy control system to raise your body well out of the water. If you have plenty of air, you can take a compass bearing and return underwater. The dive boat is a smaller target than the shore, so you need to be more careful when doing return navigation underwater. Adjust for any drift as you swim and allow for any swing of the boat around its anchor. If the boat is swinging when you take your bearing, set your course for a point between the bow and where you imagine the anchor to be resting.

Watch for any natural aids to navigation, such as rocks, wreckage, weeds, and so forth, that you passed on the way out. Also, listen for the boat's generator or compressor so you will know when you are getting close. If you swim longer than expected, surface and adjust the course. Do not swim just under the surface of the water because other boats cannot see you; instead, control your buoyancy and swim 10 to 20 feet underwater, along the bottom, or in mid-water if visibility is good.

Any ascent should be done with your buddy at a very slow, easy pace, while using buoyancy control to reduce the work of swimming. Be sure to look up, hold your hand up, go slowly, pause at 10 feet, and listen for other boats.

If you arrive back at the boat's anchor line or you have surfaced up the boat's anchor line, it is often easier to swim underwater beneath the boat directly from the anchor line to the ramp or ladder at the stern. Surface slightly behind and/or to the side of the stern and watch the wave and boat action. Be sure the area is clear before you move in and then come in with your head well above the water and take a secure hold of the ramp or ladder. Remove fins or hand up accessary gear, depending on the arrangement (platform, ramp, swim step, or ladder), as shown in figure 3-24. You should hand up spearguns butt-first. On many boat ramps, it is best to remove your fins while you are on your hands and knees. Wait for any divers ahead of you to finish climbing the ladder before you begin.

Fig. 3-24 Returning to Ramp

If you should surface down-current from the boat, you will have the current against you for the swim back. There are several choices to ease the situation:

1. Swim to the current line, as shown in figure 3-25, if it is closer than the boat and pull yourself in, hand-over-hand, being careful not to become entangled in the line. Be sure to watch the boat as you pull yourself in.
2. Swim underwater on the bottom, using a compass course.
3. Swim on the surface with the buoyancy control device inflated.
4. Signal by hand or whistle for help from the boat.
5. Swim across the current to a nearby shore, hike up-current beyond the boat and then drift or swim back to the boat.

Fig. 3-25 Using Current Line

If you should miss the boat during *drift diving*, the current line is available so you can pull yourself back in. (See figure 3-20.) Most swimming methods already mentioned are not useful in strong currents of two to eight knots. If you miss the line, inflate your buoyancy control device and wait for the boat to pick you up.

There is the remote chance that you might be left or missed by the dive boat or your own boat could drift away. This could happen from the anchor dragging, a boating or diving emergency causing the boat to move, or an inaccurate roll call. If this happens, be calm and stay with your buddy. You will be missed and a search will begin.

If you are near shore when the boat misses you, swim in and get out of the water. If you are far from land, get maximum positive buoyancy. As time passes, ditch any gear that is a hindrance, however, keep your mask, snorkel, fins, buoyancy control device, and wet suit. Stay together and in the area unless you know exactly which direction to swim to decrease the time it takes for the boat to find you.

Post-Dive

As soon as your dive is over, pack your gear away. It is easier to pack your gear when the boat is not moving. If the boat has a shower, just wash yourself, not your gear, with a quick shower, because boats have a limited supply of water. The trip back is a perfect time to clean game, sunbathe, sleep, talk, eat, or drink. Be sure you know the procedure for paying for any food, drinks, or air on the trip back. Before you leave the boat, be sure you have all your dive gear and personal belongings.

Just as the anticipation and planning for a dive is as much a part of diving as the dive itself, so is the sharing of your diving experience. Of course, you and your buddy will have the most in common to share, but all divers will have similar experiences to relate. If you have made your dives with a positive and open-minded attitude, even a difficult day with rough or dirty water can be satisfying and you can gain in your diving experience.

BOATING FOR THE OWNER/OPERATOR

Boating and diving have a great deal in common. Both are demanding, yet rewarding activities and an effective blend of them can increase your recreational pleasure. Training, proper equipment, skill, experience, and planning are vital in boating and diving; while communications, rescue, first aid, weather, and navigation are also common to both activities.

U.S. COAST GUARD REQUIREMENTS

The Coast Guard does not require private boats or the operators of private boats to be licensed unless you are carrying passengers for hire. It is important to remember that fines can be very heavy if you carry passengers for hire without the proper license. Certain equipment and other actions are required by the Coast Guard and other government agencies. The nature and number of these required items vary with the size and type of boat. The following categories are included:

1. Boat registration and numbering
2. Accident reporting
3. Rules of the road
4. Boat ventilation
5. Pollution control
6. Personal flotation devices (See figure 3-26.)
7. Fire extinguishers (See figure 3-27.)
8. Back-fire flame control
9. Signal equipment (See figure 3-28.)
10. Navigation lights

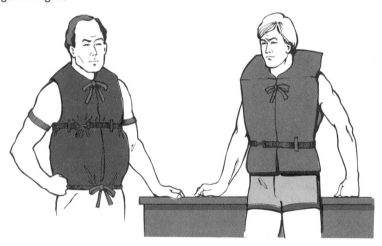

Fig. 3-26 Personal Flotation Devices

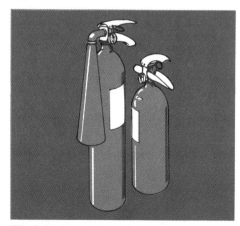

Fig. 3-27 Fire Extinguishers

Fig. 3-28 Signal Equipment

EQUIPMENT

If you own a boat and use it for diving, there is some additional boating and diving equipment you should consider carrying. What you actually decide to carry depends on the size of the boat, the area of operation, and the type of diving activities. Remember, diving equipment can also be used to solve boating problems, such as untangling a propeller or anchor or searching for equipment lost overboard.

Boating safety and first aid equipment includes:

First aid kit and book
Oxygen
Fire extinguishers
Personal flotation devices
Signal equipment
Flares
Bailing or pumping equipment
Blankets

Diving operation and support equipment includes:

Current line and float
Extra floats
Dive flag
Diving spare parts and repair kit
Extra scuba unit and weights
Lines for tying off gear and for decompression
Extra mask, snorkel, and fins
Decompression tables
Open water diving textbook
Diving emergency information
Book of local dive site information

Boat operation and support equipment includes:

Radio
Compass
Anchors and lines
Ladder
Tie-down lines for gear
Engine spare parts
Tools
Extra lines
Boating publications and charts
Knife
Boat hook
Flashlight
Fathometer

Comfort and convenience equipment includes:

Trash container
Motion sickness medication
Towels and rags
Water

SELECTING A BOAT

Because of the tremendous variables in boats and diving, it is not possible to provide a complete review of boat selection. But if you want your own diving boat, some general ideas will help you.

Dive from a commercial dive boat in the area you intend to use your boat. Carefully observe how the boat is equipped, handled, and which dive sites are used; go boating with a friend or rent a boat and try boating in the area; and take a boating course. You can also go to local boat dealers and look over the selection.

Be aware that a private boat intended for diving should have an easy way to enter and exit the water. It should be durable and not fancy because tanks and weights are hard on boats, and it should have room for both dive gear and boat equipment. Make sure the boat is suitable for local weather and water conditions and is capable of carrying more weight than you intend to put in it. Any boat you choose should also adapt to other activities, such as water skiing, fishing, cruising, and so forth.

Having your own boat is a significant investment of your effort, time, and money. With this investment comes additional responsibilities to your passengers and other boaters. You may decide that for the investment, you are better off diving from commercial dive boats. But, if you decide that having a boat is best for you, you should be strongly committed to this combination of boating and diving. Learn all you can about these skills so you can become adept at both.

BOATING TECHNIQUES
Training

A boating course is an absolute must for the boat owner/operator. However, such a course helps any diver, particularly a boat diver. Safe boating courses are offered by the U.S. Power Squadron and the U.S. Coast Guard Auxiliary for very little charge. Much of this training applies directly to boat diving or diving in general. Activities, such as search and recovery, light salvage, underwater navigation, diver rescue, plus the varying environmental conditions of tide, current, waves, and wind are better understood after a boating course. If there is no boating course in your area, you should refer to the many books available on boating.

Navigation and Seamanship

Much of the time in boating courses is spent on various aspects of navigation and seamanship. If you have your own boat you will, of course, take one of these courses. But even if you do not have a boat, some key points will make you a better informed diver, particularly around boats.

Figure 3-29 shows part of a chart used for boating. Divers can gain much valuable underwater information from these charts. Figure 3-30 shows part of a typical tide table. Tides can have a tremendous influence on diving conditions. You should acquire one of these tables for your local area. They are often available at diving, fishing, boating, and sporting goods stores. Several useful knots that are most often used by divers are shown in figure 3-31.

If weather storm warnings, as shown in figure 3-32, are displayed, you should not go out in a boat. Diving from shore will probably not be good at these times.

Fig. 3-29 Navigation Chart Section

Fig. 3-30 Tide Tables

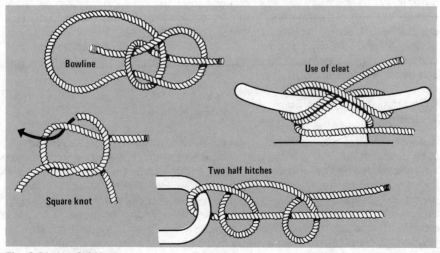

Fig. 3-31 Useful Knots

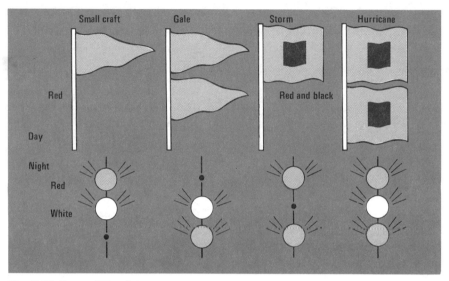

Fig. 3-32 Storm Warnings

Anchoring is another crucial skill for boating. Divers often locate lost anchors or free those which are entangled. Figure 3-33 shows several different anchors. A boat anchored for diving is shown in figure 3-34. Boats are usually anchored with only one anchor at the bow, but to keep the boat from swinging or to make it more secure, anchors are used fore and aft. Anchors used from dive boats should have a short length of chain to add weight to the anchor and prevent chafing near the anchor, as shown in figure 3-35.

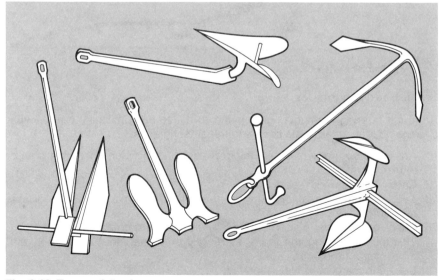

Fig. 3-33 Types of Anchors

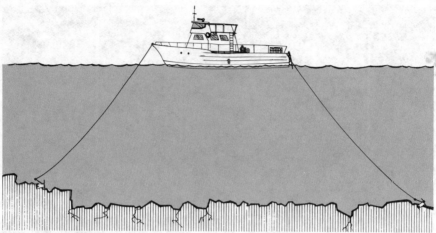

Fig. 3-34 Anchoring Fore and Aft

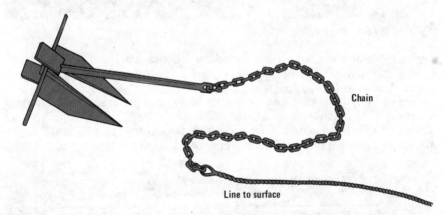

Chain

Line to surface

Fig. 3-35 Anchor with Chain

Small Boat Techniques

Although boating techniques in relation to diving are similar no matter what size the boat is, small boats have additional techniques.

1. Advise someone who is not going of your boating plan, including time of return.
2. Check the weather report.
3. Keep both dive gear and the number of divers to a safe, comfortable minimum.
4. Check out another person on the boat in case something happens to you. This includes using the radio, starting the engine, hoisting anchor, and maneuvering the boat.
5. Secure loose gear while underway.
6. If the boat is very small and the trip is short, you might suit up on shore.

7. If you put gear on while in the boat, stay low, move slowly, and be careful.
8. Anchor as near as possible to the dive site and stay out of any traffic or other hazardous areas.
9. Be sure the anchor is secure before the dive, then check the anchor when you reach the bottom.
10. Leave a person in the boat, if possible.
11. Fly the "diver down" flag only when people are actually diving.
12. If you are in a current area, put out a current line with a float.
13. Keep track of weather and sea conditions and seek shelter at the first sign of bad weather.

Fig. 3-36 Water Entry from Small Boat

The back roll is a good entry from a small boat. If the boat is very small, this should be done simultaneously by two divers on opposite sides, as shown in figure 3-36. Provide a sturdy ladder to climb out of the water or a line to tie off gear to aid in boat entries. When entering a small boat with no ladder, place accessory gear, such as spears, cameras, and so forth, carefully in the boat or tie them off. Then remove your weight belt, tank, mask, and snorkel and place them carefully into the boat one at a time. You may want to tie off your weight belt and tank. Before entering the boat, deflate your front-mounted buoyancy control device, if you are wearing one. To actually enter the boat, hold the gunwale, and give a strong kick with your fins while hoisting yourself up with your arms. (See figure 3-37.) Let your buddy help you and you should in turn help your buddy.

Fig. 3-37 Small Boat Entry

When you make a beach landing in a small boat, watch the sets of waves for some time outside the surf line. During this time, you can be strapping down equipment and checking to see that you have enough fuel. The best time to go through the surf is immediately after a big set of waves because the waves that follow will be at lower levels. This gives you time to unload and remove the motor before the next cycle of big waves.

The support and the added convenience of a boat can make your boat diving experiences some of your most memorable. This is especially true if you keep safety uppermost in your mind by using proper etiquette on board and correct techniques in the water.

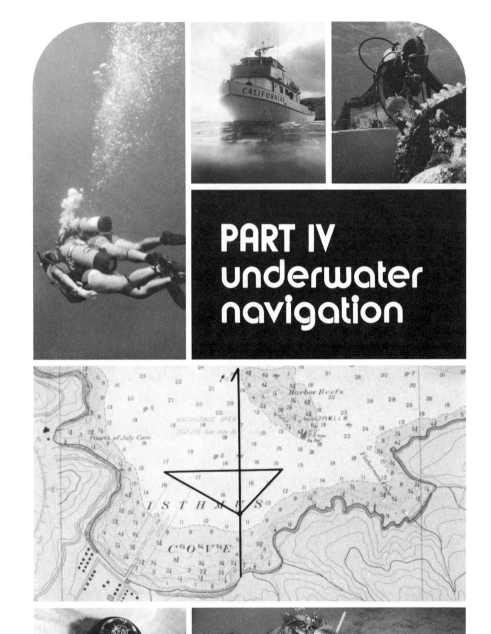

PART IV
underwater navigation

introduction

navigation had become an exacting science long before the first scuba-equipped diver broke the bonds from diving bells and air hoses, to freely explore the mysteries of the deep. But it wasn't long before the time-honored principles of seafaring navigators were applied to underwater navigation.

Navigating at depth is quite simple, in fact, most of what you need to know you have probably already experienced. Distances are the same as those on the surface, time does not change, and directions are identical to those with which you are already acquainted. The only difference is that you also have the third dimension — depth. Your diving experience is enhanced when you know where you're going and more importantly, how to get back. You will find that a basic understanding of the tools of navigation and how to properly use and interpret them instills confidence in your diving abilities.

the earth, navigation charts, compass, using charts and compass together

This material introduces a variety of navigation aids, such as charts, the function and use of the compass, as well as how to plot and swim a course under various conditions. Correctly applying these skills lets you utilize your bottom time to the utmost and dive longer with safety because you conserve your air and energy.

THE EARTH

Any serious study of navigation must eventually begin with the earth. Past navigators designed a grid system of latitude and longitude which surrounds the earth and forms the basics by which you are able to determine position.

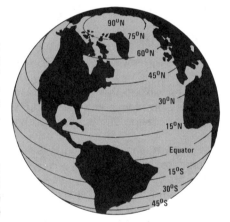

The ends of the earth's rotational axis define the geographic North and South Poles. Halfway between the poles is an imaginary line, called the equator, which divides the earth into the Northern and Southern Hemispheres. The equator is the starting,

Fig. 4-1 Lines of Latitude

or zero degree, point of latitude. Figure 4-1 illustrates that lines of latitude, or *parallels*, are evenly spaced north and south of the equator and are labeled in degrees. The poles are 90° north and south.

Lines of longitude, or *meridians,* make up the east-west references of the grid system. Through international agreement, the zero-degree longitude line, called the *prime meridian,* was established as a line running from the North and South Poles through the old Royal Observatory in Greenwich, England. From the prime meridian, the globe is divided into 180° in each direction to establish the Eastern and Western Hemispheres, as shown in figure 4-2. Early mapmakers used this simple grid system to chart the globe. Today, this system is used to accurately pinpoint positions or intended destinations on navigation charts.

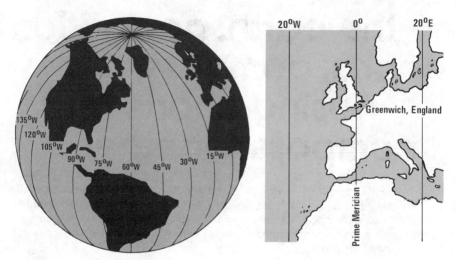

Fig. 4-2 Lines of Longitude

NAVIGATION CHARTS

Charts are nothing more than a diver's road map. When properly used, they open a whole new world of diving adventure. Charts provide detailed information about the depth of water in fathoms, shorelines, topographic features both above and below the surface, aids to navigation, dangers, and other information of interest to both navigators and divers.

There are a variety of charts available. It is important to understand the differences between each and select one most appropriate for your needs. There are four basic navigation charts of interest to divers: sailing, general, coastal, and harbor or small craft charts. Each chart, and for that matter, charts of the same type, differ in scale. Scale is the ratio of a given distance on the chart to the actual distance it represents on the earth.

Sailing charts vary in scale from 1:1,200,000 to 1:600,000. This means that one inch equals between 16 to 8 nautical miles respectively. They are used primarily for long-range seafaring navigation and provide a general overall view of certain areas. Detail is minimized and only the major topographic features are represented.

General charts range in scale between 1:600,000 and 1:100,000, or one inch is equal to approximately eight to one nautical miles respectively. They are used to plot courses along the coast and to give boaters a slightly more detailed view of a particular area.

Coastal charts range down to a scale of 1:50,000, where one inch on the chart equals a little more than one-half nautical mile. As the name implies, the charts primarily show outlying reefs, shoals, and bays or harbors of considerable width.

The charts listed so far are primarily used by the boater and are not of much value for a diver working along the shore. However, *harbor charts* or *small craft charts*, as shown in figure 4-3, have a scale from 1:50,000 down to 1:5,000, or a range from one-half mile down to where one inch equals only 139 yards. These charts depict great detail and provide the information you need to locate specific objects or diving areas.

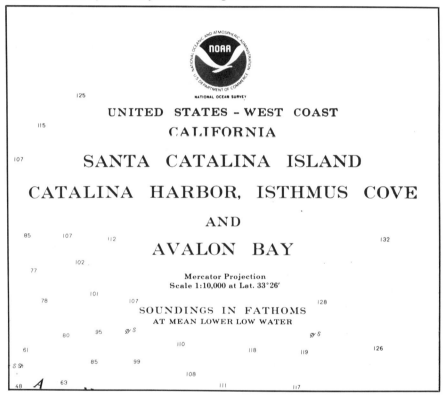

Fig. 4-3 Harbor Chart

CHART SOURCES

Several government agencies publish and sell navigation charts. The most common charts are put out by the National Oceanic and Atmospheric Administration (NOAA), the National Ocean Survey (NOS), the Defense Mapping Agencies Hydrographics Center, and the United States Lake Survey Center. Most dive shops and some Government Printing Office bookstores have catalogs available to help you select the appropriate chart.

CHART SYMBOLS

Chart information is portrayed by a set of standard symbols and color codes. To gain the maximum benefit from the chart you select, you should become familiar with its symbology.

Depth, for example, is marked in either feet or fathoms. A fathom, as you recall, is six feet. Contour lines, shown in figure 4-4, connect points of the same relative depth. In addition, the depths above 30 feet are color-coded within each zone so you can instantly recognize them. This gives you a good indication of the relative depth of any dive.

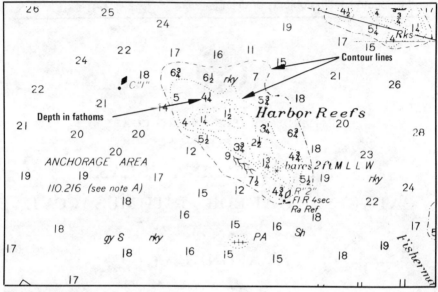

Fig. 4-4 Depth and Contour Lines

Chart symbols are also used to point out submerged and partially submerged objects and their actual depths. (See figure 4-5.) Charts show rocks and reefs, and which ones are covered and uncovered at both high and low tide. Furthermore, they indicate the type of bottom and its quality within any given area. Charts also depict reference points or landmarks which help you locate or relocate exciting dive spots.

Partially submerged wreck	Rock	Landmark	Quality of Bottom	
	⊛	⊛ Eagle Rk (rep 1955)	G	Gravel
			Sn	Shingle
			P	Pebbles
			St	Stones
			Rk; rky	Rock; Rocky
			Blds	Boulders
			Ck	Chalk

Fig. 4-5 Chart Symbols

The margins of the chart contain the degrees of latitude and longitude. Each degree is divided into 60 equal units, called *minutes*, and each minute is further subdivided into 60 *seconds*, as shown in figure 4-6. One minute of longitude represents one nautical mile, or about 6,076 feet. Determining latitude and longitude enables you to pinpoint exact locations on the chart and either relay that information to others or record the precise location of an object.

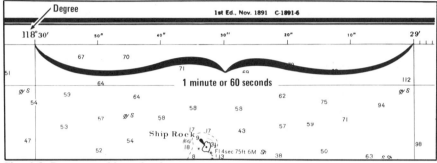

Fig. 4-6 Degrees of Longitude

Correct use of these underwater charts can greatly enhance your diving experience, not only for locating specific items, but also for the enjoyment of studying the charts and preparing for other exciting dives.

COMPASS
The key instrument to underwater navigation is the compass. To some people, the compass is a mysterious and magical instrument. The truth is that the compass is not only a simple device, but is also an essential, basic safety tool.

The main purpose of a compass is to aid in directional control. To you, this means the added ability to return to the boat, if boat diving, without surfacing to reorient yourself. This saves valuable time, energy, and effort.

A compass is particularly useful when diving from depths where stage decompression is required. It is not only impractical, it is extremely dangerous to look for the boat at the surface before you make the decompression stop. It is quite critical that you be able to return by an underwater route, relocate the boat, and remain at the required depth until it is safe to surface.

When combined with charts, the compass can help you more easily locate underwater reefs, known shipwrecks, and add more time to each dive for pleasurable exploration.

COMPASS PARTS
To understand compass function, you must first understand the parts of a compass. The original compass was nothing more than an iron needle which

a ship's pilot rubbed against a lode stone. The lode stone was a chunk of magnetized iron ore with the ability to magnetize other bits of the same metal. The magnetized needle was pushed through a piece of straw and floated in a bowl of water, as shown in figure 4-7. The magnetic attraction of the needle made it point toward the Magnetic North Pole.

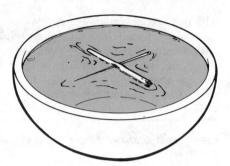

Fig. 4-7 Early Compass

Today's more sophisticated compass is much more reliable and accurate than its early predecessor. It is still, however, a relatively simple tool. Compasses come in a wide variety of shapes, sizes, and types. Let's examine the parts of a typical underwater compass, as shown in figure 4-8.

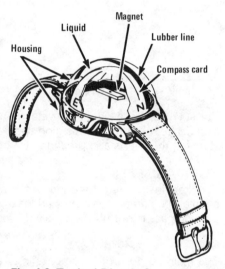

A compass card labeled with the 360 degrees of a circle is affixed to a magnet. The north, zero, or 360-degree label of the card is aligned with the centerline of the magnet. The card and magnet are suspended in a liquid-filled housing. A lubber line is permanently attached to the front of the housing. When the compass is held in the proper position, the lubber line parallels the centerline of your body.

Fig. 4-8 Typical Diver's Compass

Another familiar type of compass is shown in figure 4-9. This compass consists of a magnetic needle suspended in a liquid-filled housing. The outer ring, or bezel, depicts the degrees of a circle and is fixed in place. The lubber line is the small arrowhead at the north or zero degree position on the bezel. The two heavy bars on the face of the compass can be rotated to align with the desired course on the bezel. To maintain the selected course, you keep the magnetic needle between the bars and sight along the lubber line.

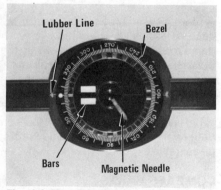

Fig. 4-9 Top-Reading
Navigation Compass

TYPES OF UNDERWATER COMPASSES

Several considerations must be kept in mind when you select a compass, such as how you intend to use it, the product's quality, how well it functions, and, of course, how much it costs. The general categories of compasses are the watchband, the wrist-mounted top-and side-reading, and the more sophisticated compass boards used primarily for competitive navigation courses. (See figures 4-10 through 4-13.)

The first thing to determine when selecting a compass is how you intend to use it. If you want one for general directional control to return to your point of entry, a simple, durable compass may be sufficient. On the other hand, if you need a compass capable of precise navigation, such as required in commercial diving or competitive compass runs, you may want the board-mounted compass. For the vast majority of divers who want dependable, reasonably priced compasses that are easy to use, one of the top-or side-reading compasses is certainly the most desirable and practical.

Watchband Compass

The watchband compass, shown in figure 4-10, provides general directional information which enables you to return to a predetermined area with a fair degree of accuracy. This type only depicts the cardinal points of a compass and should not be used for navigation in poor visibility or where a high degree of accuracy is required.

A positive aspect to the watchband compass is its small size. It is always attached to the watch and can be referred to at any moment without worrying about an additional compass or remembering to put it on or take it off. They are very durable, require almost no maintenance, and with just reasonable protection from extremely hard use, last a long time. Watchband compasses are also inexpensive.

Top-Reading Compass

The top-reading, or mariner's compass, as shown in figure 4-11, comes in a wide variety of qualitites. Your demands on the compass should determine

Fig. 4-10 Watchband Compass

Fig. 4-11 Top-Reading Navigation Compass

the quality of the compass you buy. Styles range from a very inexpensive compass with minimal quality and dependability, up to the more sophisticated compasses commonly found on boats.

A good top-reading diver's compass should have, as minimum requirements, degrees around the outside, either on the bezel, marked on the compass body itself, or on a floating compass card. It should have a movable bezel, which enables you to set a predetermined course and reciprocal, or reverse, course under readily visible points. The compass should be sensitive, but not so sensitive as to react to every metallic item along the course. The compass also should not have a significant lag or slow response. It needs to respond quickly enough so any off-course deviation is immediately noted. The compass should also have a strap or some means of securely attaching it to your body, but at the same time, it should be easy to remove in case you want to hold it for a more accurate navigation procedure.

Side-Reading Compass

The side-reading, or aviation compass, as shown in figure 4-12, is essentially the same as the top-reading compass, both in style and quality. The only difference is that it provides directional information that can be read from the side. It is also designed primarily to let you hold the compass in your hand or on your wrist in front of your face to maintain a visual line of sight while reading the compass.

Board-Mounted Compass

Fig. 4-12 Side-Reading Wrist Compass

The final type of compass used in diving is the board-mounted compass, as shown in figure 4-13. This compass is used exclusively for precision navigation, such as required in competitive navigation courses or for the commercial or military diver who must locate exactly a specific spot or return via some complex route.

Board-mounted compasses can be either a side- or top-reading compass. They are, however, of a quality generally found either on boats or airplanes and are used for cross-country navigation or cross-water navigation where extreme dependability and accuracy is an absolute requirement. Generally, they are very expensive and range in design from a simple solid-mounted, liquid-filled compass to a compass mounted on a base which stays level at all times and responds instantly to the slightest course deviation.

COMPASS CARE AND HANDLING

After a dive, the compass should be washed, cleaned, and relubricated. Remove all sand, dirt, and saltwater deposits from the case. Relubricating, in

Fig. 4-13 Board-Mounted Compass

most cases, means nothing more than simply spraying it with silicone after a thorough washing. Full attention should be given to the bezel to make sure it moves freely enough so you can adjust it underwater with gloves on, but with enough resistance so it will stay in place once you have set it.

Compasses, by their very nature, tend to be a bit fragile and as such, require careful handling, similar to a camera or watch. If your compass is to maintain its quality and dependability, the magnetic needle has to move freely. When transporting any compass, pack it carefully inside your gear bag to protect it from damage, as shown in figure 4-14. Pack and handle a board-mounted compass very carefully so it will not be thrown off the settings. Given this kind of care, your compass should last a long time and give you good, accurate, dependable service.

Fig. 4-14 Packing Compass

VARIATION

A basic consideration with a compass is that it points to the *Magnetic North Pole*, which is approximately 1,000 miles south of the *True North Pole*, as shown in figure 4-15. Therefore, when the compass points to 0° or magnetic north, it is not necessarily pointing to true north. Variation is the difference, expressed in degrees, between true north and magnetic north.

There are points within the United States where there is no variation between magnetic north to true north. This is when the True and Magnetic North Poles are in line. A line drawn through these points is called the

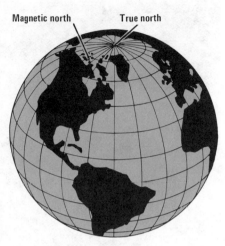

Fig. 4-15 Magnetic North

agonic line (see figure 4-16.) The compass will read 0° and there will be 0° variation. But points either east or west will have a variation, depending on how far west or east they actually are. Variation is designated as east or west on all charts, depending on whether the magnetic needle is deflected to the east or west of true north. To convert the course you draw on a chart to a magnetic course that you can follow with a compass, apply this popular saying: "east is least and west is best." This means you should subtract easterly variation and add westerly variation.

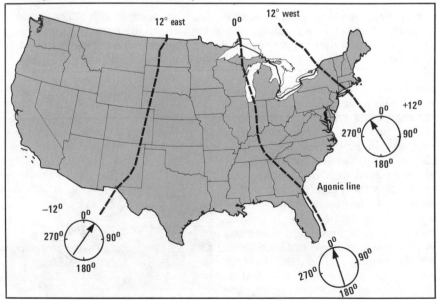

Fig. 4-16 Magnetic Variation

Two methods are commonly used for portraying variation. On small-scale charts where large distances are shown in a small area, lines that connect points of equal variation are drawn. On large-scale charts, such as those most often used by divers, a compass rose is used. (See figure 4-17.) The outer compass rose is oriented to true north, while the inner compass rose points to magnetic north. The difference between the two is the variation. The degrees of variation are also labeled in the middle of the compass rose.

Variation changes only slightly from year-to-year by the shifting of the earth's molten core. The change each year is calculated and noted on nautical charts.

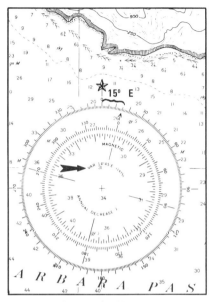

Fig. 4-17 Compass Rose

DEVIATION

Another common inherent compass error is *deviation*. Deviation is created by the magnetic interference of metallic objects within the immediate vicinity of the compass. On a boat it could be something as simple as a metal can or set of keys near the compass. While diving, deviation can occur when the compass is held too close to the mask, tank, or other gauges. For this reason, you should be aware of metallic objects around, or on you, which might create deviation. Metallic objects you pass over on the bottom could also create deviation.

Generally, you have very little control over magnetic interferences caused by metal objects on the bottom. You do, however, have control over the interference of metal objects you wear. To determine how your equipment affects your compass, arrange it on the ground and move the compass around it. You can determine which equipment has the greatest influence on the compass and the best position to hold the compass to minimize the effects of deviation.

On the surface, deviation can be accepted to a large extent because the compass generally is not relied on exclusively for directional control. You can go from one sighted point to another sighted point, or along a course where there are other objects on which you can take a heading, sometimes called a sighting, fix, or bearing. However, underwater it is sometimes impractical, if not impossible, to rely on visual sighting to maintain a course. For this reason, greater reliance on the compass is essential. Be continually on guard for deviation influence, by observing the surrounding terrain within your range of vision. You should be able to determine if you are moving in a straight line or moving at some angle to the intended course.

TIPS ON USING THE COMPASS

To use a compass underwater, take the hand that has the compass and grasp the opposite arm at the elbow. Your opposite arm should be pointing in the direction you plan to swim. (See figure 4-18.) This technique provides a solid base for the compass and aligns the lubber line or direction-of-travel arrows with the centerline of your body. This allows you to more easily follow the compass heading. Hold the compass level. When tilted too far, the compass card will no longer move freely and will drag on the compass body, preventing accurate direction control. A problem with this technique is that it quite often places the compass in immediate proximity to the mask, tank, and, in some cases, to other gauges. To minimize deviation, avoid as many metallic objects as possible.

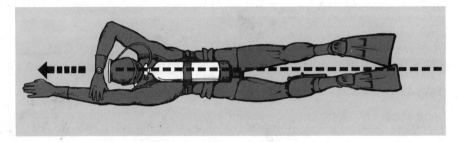

Fig. 4-18 Using the Compass

For more precise navigation, you may find it desirable to loosen the compass from the wrist and hold it out in front of you with both hands, as shown in figure 4-19. This technique provides the same solidarity as the armlock method and moves the compass far enough away from metallic items that can induce magnetic deviation. The compass can also be installed in an instrument panel, or console, which houses other gauges and meters, such as the submersible pressure gauge, depth gauge, and decompression meter.

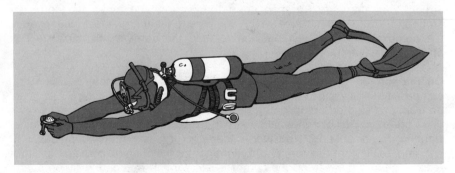

Fig. 4-19 Holding the Compass

If you are to navigate underwater accurately, the compass course must be followed exactly. This means maintaining a relationship between the compass, lubber line, and body. For example, assume you have the type of compass depicted in figure 4-20, and you want to swim a westerly course of 270°. Hold the compass with the lubber line exactly parallel to the length of your body and move until 270°, or west, is directly behind the lubber line. Maintain this relationship as you swim and you will follow a 270° heading.

If you have the type of compass shown in figure 4-21, and you want to swim the same westerly course, set the movable bracket lines on the face of the compass opposite 270° on the bezel. Then move until the compass needle is between the brackets. To maintain the heading, simply keep the compass needle between the bracket lines and sight along the lubber line. When the correct position has been established, you should think of your direction of travel as a line passing directly through your body, intersecting the compass lubber line, and pointing precisely to your destination.

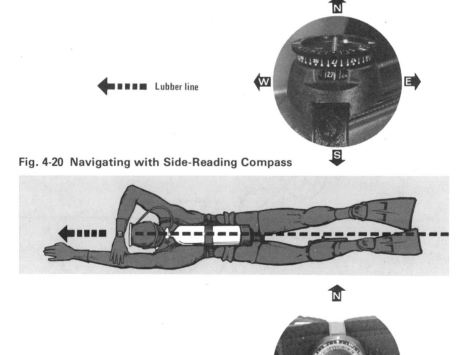

Lubber line

Fig. 4-20 Navigating with Side-Reading Compass

Lubber line

Fig. 4-21 Navigating with Top-Reading Compass

Once you understand these key relationships and have mastered a simple out course and then reciprocal dive courses, you are ready for more advanced underwater navigation techniques. These techniques can include such things as triangular courses and the more complicated techniques as used by surface navigators.

USING CHARTS AND COMPASS TOGETHER

Select a chart for the diving area of your preference. The easiest procedure when using a chart is to always turn the "north" of the chart toward true north. Then, when you draw your course line on the chart, it will be pointed in the actual direction you intend to swim.

Next, draw a line with a straightedge from your starting point to your destination. This is your *course line*. (See figure 4-22.) After you draw the line, one method you may use to navigate is to select objects along the course line, such as reefs, wrecks, shelves, buoys tied to the bottom, or other objects, and plan to swim from one object to the other. It makes no difference if they are slightly off the desired course, you can still reach your destination. This technique of using objects for checkpoints is desirable even when you swim a course by compass, because it lets you continuously monitor your progress and helps you more easily maintain the course.

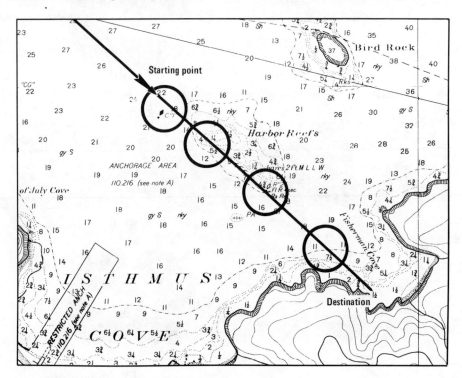

Fig. 4-22 Course Line and Checkpoints

The other method is to accurately measure the course as an angle from true north. To do this, you need a protractor, marine plotter, or an air navigation plotter, similar to the one shown in figure 4-23. Align the baseline of the plotter with the course line. Then, with the center of the plotter over a line of longitude, read the *true course* from the plotter rose. (See figure 4-24.) (Small arrows are printed on the rose to indicate the scale to be used for your direction of travel.) Double-check your answer by mentally visualizing the general direction of the course.

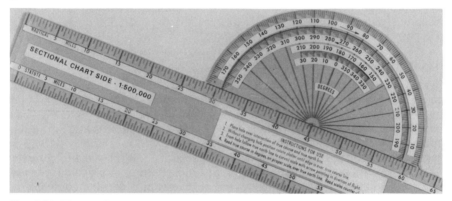

Fig. 4-23 Navigation Plotter

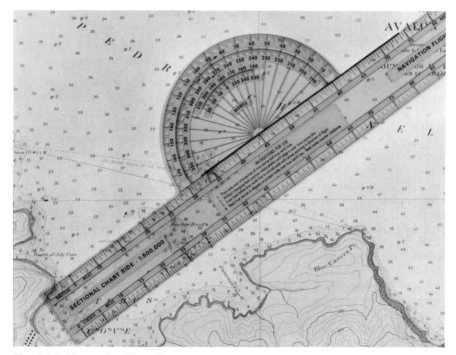

Fig. 4-24 Measuring True Course

At times, the course line may not cross a line of longitude. To determine the true course, simply extend the course line until it intersects a line of longitude. Then use the procedure just described to find the true course.

Next, add or subtract the magnetic variation for the area. The amount of variation is obtained by reading the value from the nearest variation line or compass rose nearest your course line. (You may have to interpolate it if necessary for your position on the chart.) The value you have after subtracting or adding variation is called the *magnetic course*. If you do not have to compensate for currents or tide, this value is the heading you set on your compass. It is called the *magnetic heading*.

RECIPROCAL DIVE COURSES

Before you can compute a reciprocal dive course, (coming back on the same course line you went out on) you must first determine the compass heading for the outbound course. For example, assume the outbound course is 290° (west/northwest). The return, reciprocal, or inbound course is 180° from the outbound course. In this case, it would be 110°, (290° −180° = 110°), or east/southeast. Because the outbound course is 290°, it is easiest to subtract 180°. If the outbound course is less than 180°, the proper precedure would be to add 180°. By predetermining these figures and setting the compass on 290°, you can follow the compass heading out and enjoy the dive. To return to the boat, set the compass on 110° and follow it back. The more computations you can do before a dive, the more you will enjoy the actual dive.

ADVANCED NAVIGATION

Currents

When you dive, you become a part of your environment and are affected by its movements. This means that as the water moves, you move, or drift with it. For example, if you maintain a northerly heading while diving in a one-knot (one nautical mile per hour) current from the east, you will drift with the current, or westward. (See figure 4-25.) In fact, after one hour, you will be one nautical mile to the west of your intended course. To compensate, you must turn *into* the current to a heading that will let the current drift you along the desired course line.

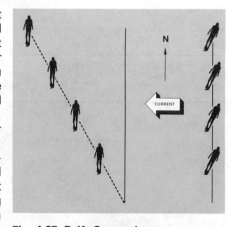

Fig. 4-25 Drift Correction

To dive in waters with current you must know two additional factors: the speed and direction of the current and your underwater swimming speed. Tidal and current tables, and tidal current charts are available from the

National Ocean Survey. Through their use and actual observations, you can determine current speed and direction fairly accurately.

To determine your swimming speed, swim a predetermined course over the bottom and either count the number of kicks to establish a feet-per-kick speed, or time the course and determine your feet-per-minute speed. The latter of the two is the most accurate for navigational purposes. The course should be repeated several times to achieve an accurate swim rate.

To determine the compass heading that compensates for the current, use a simple vector diagram, or a diagram which shows course or compass direction. You can draw this diagram on the navigation chart or on a separate piece of paper. The important item is to establish a true north line.

The first step is to plot and measure the true course. As shown in figure 4-26, the true course from point A to point B is 300°. The direction and speed of the current is plotted next. Always use the same unit of measure to plot speeds.

In this example, the current is from 225° and the speed is 1 knot. To make the speed easier to plot, 1 nautical mile per hour is converted to 1.69 feet per second (6,076 feet ÷ 3,600 seconds = 1.69 feet/second). From point A, the current line is drawn in the direction of flow. The length of this line to point C is the speed of the current, 1.69 feet second (see figure 4-26).

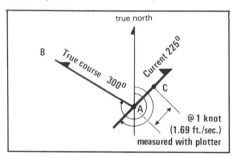

Fig. 4-26 True Course, Current Direction and Speed

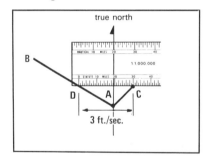

Fig. 4-27 Plotting Swim Rate

The next item to enter is your own swim speed, which we will assume to be 180 feet per minute. This value is converted to 3 feet per second (180 feet ÷ 60 seconds = 3 feet/second). The same scale on the plotter is used to plot the swim speed. You may use either scale as long as it is the same one you used to measure the length of the current line, and you continue to use the same scale for all measurements. Place 3 over point C and move the zero mark on the plotter until it intercepts the true course line, (A, B), as shown in figure 4-27.

The angle formed by the true north line and the swim speed line, (C, D), is the true heading for the dive, 269°. (See figure 4-28.) The drift correction angle is 31° left, into the current (A, C, D). Variation is then applied to this heading to achieve the compass heading for the dive.

The length of the line from point A to point D is the speed over the bottom you will maintain under these conditions. In this case, it is 2.1 feet per second. (See figure 4-28.) This speed is used to calculate how long it will take you to swim to your destination. In this example, assume the distance from A to B is 600 feet. Use the basic formula (distance ÷ speed = time) to compute the swim time. The distance, 600 feet, is divided by the speed over the bottom, 2.1 feet per second, to find the swim time of 285.7 seconds or about 4 minutes, 45 seconds.

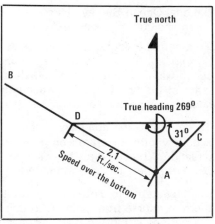

Fig. 4-28 True Heading
and Over-the-Bottom Speed

Reciprocal Courses in Currents

When you have computed your compass heading to your destination in a current, simply planning the return on a reciprocal heading will put you considerably off-course. The correction you held *into* the current on the way out will be matched by a correction into the current on the way back.

The reciprocal course must be computed from the true course and the correction angle applied to it, but in the opposite direction. In the previous example, the true course was 300°. The reciprocal course, therefore, will be 120° (300° − 180° = 120°). The correction angle was 31° left to compensate for the one knot current from the left. Since the current will be from the right on the return trip, it is added to 120°. The true heading for the return trip is 151°. Again, variation must be applied to arrive at a compass heading for the return dive.

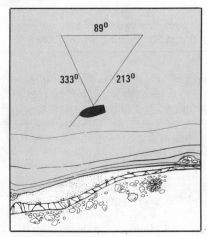

Fig. 4-29 Triangular Course

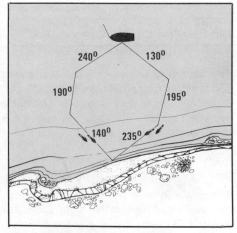

Fig. 4-30 Multiple Course Dive

Multiple Courses

Once you feel comfortable with computing navigation courses, reciprocals, and current problems, the next step is to work with routes that follow more than two headings. In a triangular course, you follow three different headings to return to the original point of departure. (See figure 4-29.) Another navigation problem you may encounter is one in which you have two groups of divers who are following separate courses and who want to meet at a predetermined point. (See figure 4-30.)

Each dive requiring navigation skills is computed using the same basic navigation techniques described earlier. Once a specific course has been plotted, the compass headings and swim times are computed separately for each leg. With more than one course to follow, it is helpful to write each compass heading and swim time on your slate for quick reference.

Search and Recovery

This specialty type of diving requires a great deal of skill, accuracy, training, and coordination. If you are not experienced or are unfamiliar with the rules of search and recovery, don't try it. As a general rule, you must be an excellent navigator, both at the surface and below; be able to coordinate search patterns, regardless of the number of divers or the visibility; and be thoroughly familiar with the techniques of safely rigging and raising objects of all sizes to the surface.

An understanding of *simple* search and recovery techniques can help you find a piece of equipment that has accidentally gone overboard. Leave the heavy search and recoveries to the professionals.

Your odds of success are increased if you follow three simple rules: define the search area, select the best search pattern, and establish a system of keeping track of the areas that have already been searched. Bearings or coordinates can be used to define the basic search area, and where to anchor. Currents or tidal movement are sometimes factors that should be considered.

The search pattern you select depends, to a large part, on the number of divers involved and environmental conditions. It could be a simple compass course or an elaborate gang sweep of the area. (See figure 4-31.) The important factor is to keep it as simple as possible. Once a certain area is searched, have a system of checking it off. This eliminates excessive overlap and duplication.

When you have located an object that is too large for you to retrieve alone, mark its location. Buoys are the best method for marking location. You will most likely have spent a lot of time and effort to locate this object and surfacing before the location is marked means you may have to spend as much time relocating it.

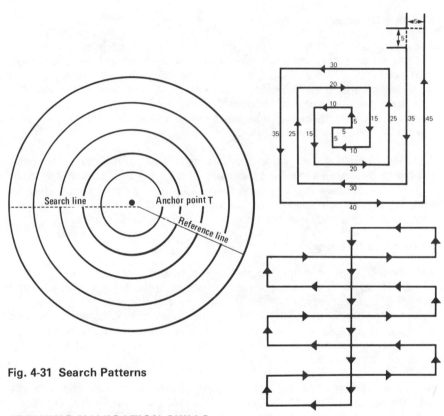

Fig. 4-31 Search Patterns

APPLYING NAVIGATION SKILLS

To see the practical application of using charts and compasses, let's follow a typical buddy team from the time they are at home planning a weekend dive through the actual dive. With charts scattered from one end of the living room to the other, they evaluate the places they have been and the places they might go, and try to decide where to dive this weekend. Eventually, they come across a chart of Santa Catalina Island and a harbor chart of Isthmus Cove on Catalina. (See figure 4-32.) They decide that this is the place, since they know of a previously lost anchor and two other intriguing areas near Bird Rock in this area.

Pre-dive Planning

When they arrive at the Isthmus, they plot their dive plan on the chart for future reference and begin the actual preparation for the dive. Using a harbor chart, they first plot the true course from the Isthmus Landing to a spot 50 yards northwest of Bird Rock where they plan to anchor. (See figure 4-33.) They find the true course to be 040°, north/northeast. The variation, as indicated on the charts, is 14°45' east, which is rounded off to 15°. (See figure 4-34.) Subtracting this from the true course gives a compass heading of 025°. The chart also indicates a depth of 12 feet at the planned anchorage. They load their gear into the boat and head to the dive site.

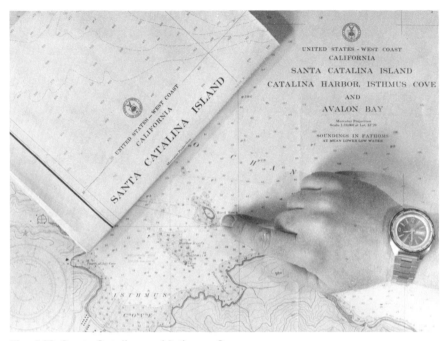

Fig. 4-32 Santa Catalina and Isthmus Cove

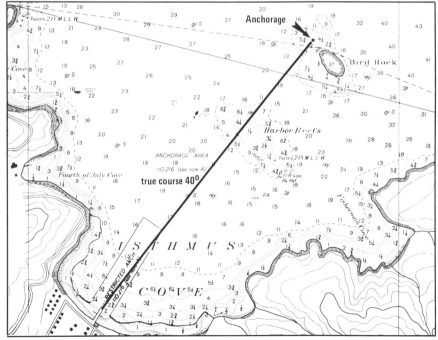

Fig. 4-33 True Course to Anchorage

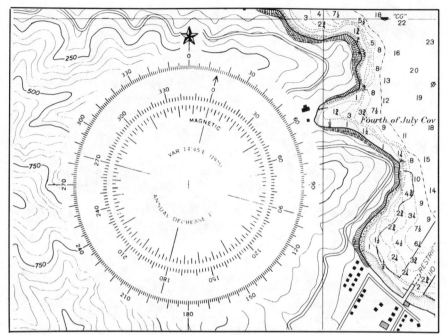

Fig. 4-34 Magnetic Variation Compass Rose

Once anchored, they begin the pre-dive checklist, using their diving log. First, they make note of the actual location of the anchorage near Bird Rock. The true course from the Isthmus was 040°, and by taking a bearing from the rocks on the northwest corner of Bird Rock, they determine the exact location to be 33°27'6"N, 117°29'14"W. The distance from the Isthmus landing is approximately 1,520 yards. (See figure 4-35.) They also note the conditions at the anchorage. The weather is beautiful and sunny, the water is calm, there is no current, and they have more than 100-foot visibility with a water temperature of 70°F and an air temperature of 85°F.

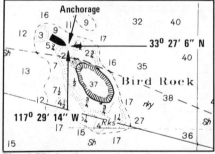

Fig. 4-35 Anchorage Location

They now begin to plot their actual dive courses. The first destination will be the mound or rise on the bottom just north of Bird Rock. (See figure 4-36.) The true course is 040°, which was the same as the course from the Isthmus landing. Since they do not have to compensate for current, they simply subtract the variation of 15° east and arrive at a compass heading of 025°. The distance to the mound is computed to be 100 yards. They each have previously determined their swim rate to be 60 feet per minute. With the distance and swim rate known, they are able to estimate the time required to reach the mound. After converting the swim rate to 20 yards per minute, (60 feet/minute ÷ 3 feet = 20 yards/minute), they compute that it will take 5 minutes to swim 100 yards (100 yards ÷ 20 yards/minute = 5 minutes).

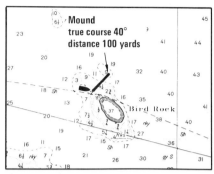

Fig. 4-36 Course to the Mound

The next step is to find how much air they will use to reach the mound. The depth of the mound is 9 fathoms, which converts to 54 feet. They estimate that the average depth during the dive will be 30 feet and their surface air consumption rate is 25 psi per minute. Referring to the air consumption tables, they note that with a surface consumption rate of 25 psi per minute, their air consumption rate at 30 feet will be 47.5 psi per minute. For five minutes, they will use 237.5 psi. The information for this leg is entered in the dive log.

On the second leg of the dive, they will try to locate the lost anchor. They estimate its position and draw the true course. (See figure 4-37.) The anchor should be 100 yards south/southeast of the mound on a true course of 162°. The magnetic heading will be 147°. At a swim rate of 20 yards per minute, it will take 5 minutes to reach the anchor. The planned average depth for this leg is again 30 feet and the air consumption is calculated to be 237.5 psi. This information is written on the dive log.

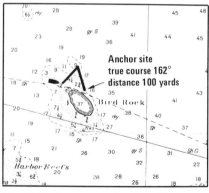

Fig. 4-37 Course to Anchor Site

The third leg of the dive will be the return trip to the boat. (See figure 4-38.) From the estimated location of the lost anchor to the boat, the true course is 284° and the magnetic heading is 266°. The distance is 100 yards and again, it will take 5 minutes to complete this. Due to the rapidly rising terrain on the return trip, they estimate their average depth to be 15 feet. From the air consumption table, they determine the air consumption rate at 36.3 psi per minute. For the last leg, they will use 181.5 psi.

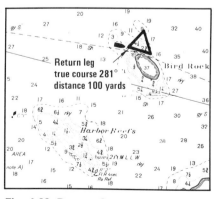

Fig. 4-38 Return Course

ISTHMUS LANDING TO ANCHORAGE
True Course - 40°
Compass Heading - 25°
Distance - 1,520 Yards

LEG-1 TO MOUND
True Course - 40°
Compass Heading - 25°
Distance - 100 Yards
Dive Time - 5 Minutes
Average Depth - 30 Feet
Air Consumed - 237.5 p.s.i.
Time at the Mound.

LEG-2 TO THE ANCHOR
True Course - 162°
Compass Heading - 147°
Distance - 100 Yards
Dive Time - 5 Minutes
Average Depth - 30 Feet
Air Consumed - 237.5 p.s.i.
Time at the Anchor.

LEG-3 RETURN TO THE BOAT
True Course - 281°
Compass Heading - 266°
Distance - 100 Yards
Dive Time - 5 Minutes
Average Depth - 15 Feet
Air Consumed - 181 p.s.i.

Fig. 4-39 Course Planning

With the course planning complete, as shown in figure 4-39, the divers now determine how much time they will be able to spend at each destination, based on the total air volume of their tanks. Each diver has 3,000 psi of air. The air consumed on each leg is added for a total of 656.5 psi. They also want to return to the boat with a reserve of at least one-third of their total air supply, which is 1,000 psi. This is added to the air consumed during the swim for a total of 1,656.5 psi. This figure is subtracted from the total air pressure of the tank, which leaves a total of 1,343.5 psi of air to be divided between the mound and looking for the anchor.

Both divers agree that they would like to spend as much time as possible at both sites and that looking for the anchor may take a little longer. Therefore, they decide to spend 10 minutes at the mound and 13 minutes looking for the anchor.

With the top of the mound at a depth of 54 feet, they assume that most of their time will be spent at around 60 feet. Their air consumption rate at 60 feet is 70 psi per minute. For a 10-minute dive at this depth, they will consume 700 psi. The average depth in the area of the lost anchor is 30 feet and at this depth, their air consumption rate is 47.5 psi per minute. The total consumed in 13 minutes will be 617.5 psi. The total air consumed at both dive sites is 1,317.5 psi, which is well within the total air available. They recheck all of their calculations. (See figure 4-40.)

The Dive

Having detailed the dive plan, they finish their pre-dive checklist in the log. First, they dress and check each other for correct equipment adjustment. (See figure 4-41.) As shown in figure 4-42, they note in their logs the size of their tanks, which are 72 cu. foot, 3,000 psi and that their starting psi is exactly 3,000 psi for each of them.

DIVE CALCULATION

LEG I TO MOUND
TRUE COURSE - 40°
VARIATION - 15° E
CURRENT - 0
DISTANCE - 100 YDS.
AVG. DEPTH - 30 FT.
SURFACE AIR CONSUMPTION RATE -
25 PSI PER MIN.
SWIM RATE - 60 FT. PER MIN.

COMPASS HEADING = TC 40° - 15° EV = 25°
TIME TO MOUND =
1. CONVERT 60 FPM TO YDS PER MIN. =
60 ÷ 3 = 20 YDS. PER MIN.
2. DISTANCE 100 YDS. ÷ 20 YPM = 5 MINUTES
AIR CONSUMED =
1. FROM AIR CONSUMPTION TABLES, CONSUMPTION RATE AT
DEPTH OF 30 FT. FOR A SURFACE CONSUMPTION RATE
OF 25 PSI PER MIN. IS 47.5 PSI PER MIN.
5 MIN × 47.5 PSI PER MIN = 237.5 PSI

LEG II TO ANCHOR
TRUE COURSE - 162°
VARIATION - 15° E
CURRENT - 0
DISTANCE - 100 YDS.
AVG. DEPTH - 30 FT.
SURFACE AIR CONSUMPTION RATE -
25 PSI PER MIN.
SWIM RATE - 60 FT. PER MIN.

COMPASS HEADING = TC 162° - 15° EV = 147°
TIME TO MOUND = (SAME CALCULATION AS LEG I)

LEG III RETURN TO BOAT
TRUE COURSE - 281°
VARIATION - 15° E
CURRENT - 0
DISTANCE - 100 YDS.
AVG. DEPTH - 15 FT.
SURFACE AIR CONSUMPTION RATE -
25 PSI PER MIN.
SWIM RATE - 60 FT. PER MIN.

COMPASS HEADING = TC 281° - 15° EV = 266°
TIME TO MOUND =
1. CONVERT 60 FPM TO YDS. PER MIN. =
60 FPM ÷ 3 = 20 YDS PER MIN.
2. DISTANCE 100 YDS. ÷ 20 YDS PER MIN. = 5 MIN.
AIR CONSUMED =
1. FROM AIR CONSUMPTION TABLES, CONSUMPTION RATE AT
DEPTH OF 15 FT. FOR A SURFACE CONSUMPTION RATE OF
25 PSI PER MIN. IS 36.3 PSI PER MIN.
5 MIN. × 36.3 PSI PER MIN. = 181.5 PSI PER MIN.

AIR CONSUMED:
1. FROM AIR CONSUMPTION TABLES, CONSUMPTION RATE AT
DEPTH OF 15 FT. FOR A SURFACE CONSUMPTION RATE OF
25 PSI PER MIN. IS 36.3 PSI PER MIN.
5 MIN × 36.3 PSI PER MIN. = 181.5 PSI PER MIN.

TOTAL AIR CONSUMED FOR 3 LEGS =
237.5 PSI PER MIN.
237.6 PSI PER MIN.
181.5 PSI PER MIN.

948 TOTAL   656.5 PSI
PLUS RESERVE   + 1000.0 PSI
                  1656.5 PSI

TOTAL IN TANKS 3000.0 PSI
             - 1656.5 PSI
                1343.5 PSI REMAINING TO USE AT MOUND
                          AND LOST ANCHOR SITE.

• MOUND -
10 MIN. AT AVG. DEPTH OF 60 FT. WITH A CONSUMPTION RATE
OF 70 PSI PER MIN. = 70 PSI PER MIN. × 10 MIN. = 700 PSI PER MIN.
• LOST ANCHOR -
13 MIN. AT AVG. DEPTH OF 50 FT. WITH A AIR CONSUMPTION
RATE OF 47.5 PSI PER MIN. = 47.5 PSI PER MIN. × 13 MIN. =
617.5 PSI

617.5 PSI + 700 PSI = 1317.5 PSI.
1343.5 PSI REMAINING AIR
- 1317.5 PSI PROJECTED USE
  26.0 PSI SURPLUS TO ADD TO RESERVE

Fig. 4-40 Rechecking Calculations

Fig. 4-41 Checking Equipment

DATE_____
DIVE LOCATION: _CATALINA ISLAND, ISTHMUS, BIRD ROCK_
DIRECTIONS: _1520 YDS. 40° NNE FROM ISTHMUS LANDING_
COORDINATES: _____

CONDITIONS:

WEATHER	SURFACE	CURRENT	VISIBILITY	
☑ Sunny	☑ Calm	☑ None	☑ Excellent	WATER TEMPERATURE _70°_
☐ Cloudy	☐ Choppy	☐ Light	☐ Good	
☐ Overcast	☐ Rough	☐ Medium	☐ Poor	AIR TEMPERATURE _85°_
☐ Stormy	☐ Stormy	☐ Heavy	☐ None	

DIVE BUDDY(S) _RON BLAKE_

PRE-DIVE CHECK LIST

BUDDY GEAR CHECK	SAFETY PROCEDURE	TIME IN:		(YOU)	(BUDDY)
☑ Adjustment	☑ Depth				
☑ Buckle Location	☑ Minimum PSI Prior to Surfacing (500)	_10:05_	Tank Size	_72_	_72_
☑ Octopus	☑ Direction 25° NNE, 147° SSE	TIME OUT:	PSI Start	_3,000_	_3,000_
☑ Air On	☑ Compass Heading 266° NNW		PSI Return		
	☑ Lost Buddy Procedure				

REPETITIVE DIVE CALCULATIONS

Depth	Bottom Time	Repetitive Group	Surface Time	New Depth	New Group	No Decomp Time

WITNESS:_____

DIVE NARRATIVE (use back for complete details)

Fig. 4-42 Dive Log

Fig. 4-43 The Mound

Fig. 4-44 Taking Photographs

They then note the time (10:05), enter the water and swim the 025° magnetic heading to the mound. Five minutes later, they arrive at the top of the mound, check the depth gauges and note that they are at 54 feet. (See figure 4-43.) They move down to a maximum of 60 feet where they take pictures of some lobsters. At exactly 10:15, they start for the area of the lost anchor along a magnetic heading of 147°.

When they arrive at the anchor site five minutes later, they start a circular search pattern. The anchor is located in a few minutes and they tie it to an inflatable buoy to mark the location so they can retrieve it on a second dive. They finish their 13 minutes by taking more photographs. (See figure 4-44.)

At 10:33, they reset their compasses to 266° and head back to the boat. After 5 minutes, they find themselves directly under the boat. Because there is no current, and the dive has been particularly restful, they find they have 1,250 psi left in their tanks. So, they decide to dive under the boat until they are down to 500 psi reserve, at which time they surface.

Upon surfacing, they remove their weight belts, tanks, and fins, climb into the boat, and immediately finish their log. They note their psi on return is 500 psi for the first buddy and 600 psi for the second buddy. They complete their dive profile and after a rest, they can move back to pick up the anchor, knowing precisely what their repetitive dive schedule should be.

By following this procedure, the divers are able to complete their dive with absolute safety without surfacing. They were able to go directly to each dive site, spend their allotted time, and return well within predetermined safety limits. They achieved their purpose on the dive, and prevented any undue or excess exertion. They were able to enjoy the dive itself, along with enjoying the anticipation of the dive through pre-dive planning.

Planning each dive can add a whole new dimension to your diving skills. It can help eliminate a "hit or miss" dive, add hours of pre-dive enjoyment, help you relocate good dive sites, and best of all, can add that important margin of safety that makes a dive more than "just fun."

Once these skills have been mastered, you are availed of an entirely new activity in sport diving. You can use charts to locate new and exciting diving spots. You can move to and from any predetermined location, based on simple navigational techniques without the necessity of surfacing to reorient. Diving in general becomes not only more fun, but much safer, giving you a new sense of capability. Navigation also opens up a potentially new area of the sport for competition or just pure enjoyment. The basics are simple and enjoyable and all they require is practice.

PART V
limited
visibility
diving

introduction

It would be wonderful if all the waters of the world were clear, clean, and completely free of natural and man-made pollution. If that were the case, every dive would be like swimming in an aquarium with nearly unlimited visibility. It would be great, but unfortunately, these conditions do not exist everywhere. Water in some parts of the world, particularly fresh water, has poor visibility. Sometimes, you can see no more than a few inches, and yet people regularly dive in this type of water. Other divers shun the light of day and wait until the moon rises before they slip beneath the surface of the water. What posseses these people, who would want to dive in "dirty" water or at night, and why?

Divers who see no worth in limited visibility diving are missing a unique experience. Things are different in limited visibility. Creatures act differently than they do in clear water and often there are even different creatures. A new world opens to the diver on each dive because a move of only a few feet offers a whole new realm.

turbid water.
diving in turbid water.
water at night.
night diving

One of the most important environmental factors that affects your diving activities is underwater visibility. It can range from more than 300 feet to zero. Specific examples of visibility are a range of 75 to 150 feet in the Bahamas and an average of less than 30 feet in the Great Lakes.

To dive safely in limited visibility, there are certain special considerations. You need to know what makes water "dirty" and how to recognize it. Before entering this type of water, you must have the correct equipment and a thorough dive plan. Once you are in the water, your knowledge and training will help you use the right procedures for limited visibility diving. Your procedures must be tighter, your plans better, and your senses keener than when diving in clear water. Night diving is in a class by itself, although you use similar techniques for both diving in turbid water and at night. Pre-dive planning and safety requirements are especially important for a successful night dive. A calm attitude is essential for limited visibility diving, but if you are equal to the challenge it offers, the rewards are high.

TURBID WATER

To experience both the pleasures and problems of turbid water, it is necessary to understand what turbid water really is. Low visibility water is referred to as "turbid" because it contains not only dirt, but also has a variety of matter suspended in it which causes the loss of visibility.

When the water is truly dirty, several things may be occurring. Surface winds stir the bottom and create suspended dirt or sand. Runoff from rain carries loose particles into the water. During runoff, it is best to avoid coves and bays and to dive upcurrent from streams and rivers or to dive elsewhere. Turbid water can also be caused by offshore currents and waves disturbing the bottom near shore. You find the best visibility around islands or reefs some distance from shore when visibility near the shore is low. The clearest water for diving is also located on leeward shores, away from harbors, on rocky shores with little surf, and on shores where the bottom drops quickly. (See figure 5-1.)

Tidal changes in the ocean can affect visibility. When tides change drastically, the high tide disturbs much of the bottom and material far up on

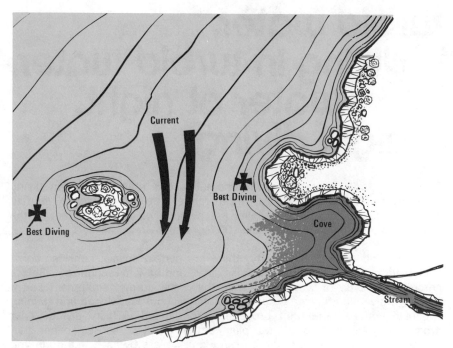

Fig. 5-1 Best Diving During Runoff

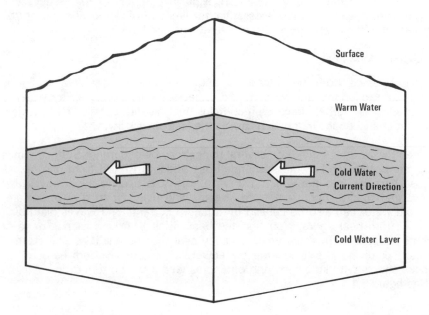

Fig. 5-2 Thermoclines

the beach. Extreme low tides create a layer of debris along the bottom which remains during the next high tide and destroys visibility right on the bottom where you want the best visibility. Tides also move shore pollution out to sea. Before diving off coasts, you should always ask local divers about tidal conditions and check the tide tables.

Thermoclines, or layers of water having different temperatures, can cause turbidity. Cold, dense water holds particles in suspension. Quite often, clear water lies immediately above or below the thermocline, depending on whether particles of dirt or some form of life are suspended in it. Sometimes there may be several horizontal thermoclines, particularly in the ocean, with alternating layers of warm and cold water, as well as clear and turbid water. (See figure 5-2.)

Fig. 5-3 Pollution

Any form of pollution also creates turbidity. (See figure 5-3.) The pollution may stem from sewage outlets, chemical spills, drainage from a variety of outflows, or dredging in the immediate area. Rivers generally produce significant amounts of silt, either when they spill into freshwater lakes or into the ocean. They also carry a great deal of suspended matter, such as microscopic life forms.

Strong surface winds can also cause currents strong enough to mix layers of water. A wind blowing in the right direction can make surface waters flow away from shore and colder bottom waters replace them. This phenomenon is called *upwelling*. Because of nutrient-rich waters rising from the bottom, upwellings are often associated with huge increases in the plankton population, and corresponding decreases in visibility.

LIFE FORMS

Turbidity in both fresh water and salt water is not caused only by suspended dirt; it can also be caused by suspended microscopic life forms. Water containing these life forms can create the illusion of being perfectly clear from the surface, however, when you dive in it, you are unable to see because the tiny organisms reflect and scatter the light. This makes the water appear "dirty." (See figure 5-4.)

Fresh Water

In fresh water, the life forms are primarily algae. Algae resembles freshwater plankton. The quantity of algae or freshwater plankton varies according to the time of the year. Generally, right after the spring thaw or before the sun warms the water in the summer, fresh water contains little or no algae. As the summer progresses, the water warms, the algae grows, and the life forms increase. This decreases visibility. As the water cools in the fall, the life forms begin to die and during the winter, they disappear.

Fig. 5-4 Light Scattering by Organisms

Salt Water

The seas are rich with plankton. The amount of plankton affecting visibility varies from season to season and from year to year. When plankton increases dramatically, it is called a "red tide." The red tide decreases visibility and, in some cases, may make diving entirely impossible.

DIVING IN TURBID WATER

You need to consider three things when you dive in turbid water. These are: visibility, direction control, and the dive plan.

VISIBILITY

Decreased visibility affects not only how far you can see, it also affects the amount of light that penetrates the water. However, you can still see better in limited visibility water when the most sunlight is available. Because light is absorbed quite rapidly at any depth over a few feet, particularly in fresh water, you may need to use an underwater light, as shown in figure 5-5. However, depending on the amount of suspended matter in the water, the light may be of little value primarily because the light hits particles of suspended matter and is reflected off at an angle equal to the approach angle. (See figure 5-6.) This is sometimes called "scatter." It affects your vision because it prevents the light from travelling very far and because there is little reflected light coming back into your eyes.

Fig. 5-5 Use of Underwater Light   **Fig. 5-6 Scatter**

To make the underwater light useful in turbid water, you need to know how to hold it. On land, of course, you simply hold the light in the most comfortable position and point it directly at an object. However, when you are underwater, you must hold the light so the reflections from the particles are scattered in directions which do not affect your ability to see. The best position, as shown in figure 5-7, is to hold the light either above or to the side of the object. This lets the light reflect off both the suspended matter and the object itself, while giving you maximum illumination.

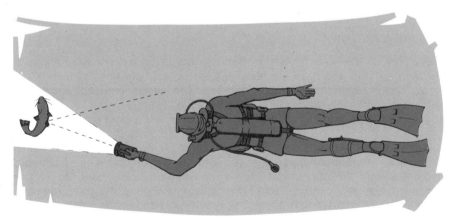

Fig. 5-7 Light Position

In turbid water, the underwater light only replaces lost surface light in the *immediate* vicinity. If visibility prevents vision beyond a few inches or feet, the light may increase your ability to perceive objects within that limit, but it does not extend your vision range beyond what the turbidity permits. (See figure 5-8.)

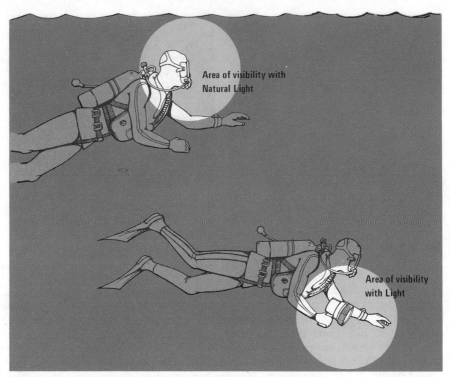

Fig. 5-8 Vision Range with Underwater Light

DISORIENTATION

The ability of the human body to function correctly and precisely depends partly upon your ability to correctly determine your position relative to the earth. This is especially important in diving. The sensations used to maintain balance are primarily from the eyes, the nerve endings in the muscles and around the joints, and certain tiny balance organs in the inner ear structure.

When you enter turbid water, you can no longer perceive the usual visual references. Subsequently, you are unable to tell "which end is up" from your nerve endings' sensations and from your balance organs' signals. This is because these nerve endings and balance organs depend, for the most part, upon a correct orientation to the pull of gravity and underwater, they may not be oriented in the same direction as gravity. The brain struggles to decipher signals sent from the senses, but without the clue normally supplied by vision, incorrect or conflicting interpretations may result.

Disorientation is intensified when sunlight comes through the water and bounces off the particles, as shown in figure 5-9. When this occurs, the light seems to concentrate along a very narrow path, causing tunnel vision. This can distort your vision and can affect how your eyes focus, as well as af-

Fig. 5-9 Sun Bouncing Off Suspended Particles

fecting your peripheral vision. The result of such sensory confusion is a dizzy, whirling sensation called *vertigo*, sometimes referred to as spacial disorientation. Vertigo may take a variety of forms. It can cause high stress levels if you are unprepared to cope with it. In some extreme cases, it causes unreasonable fear and can occasionally result in nausea.

Tunnel vision and vertigo should be overcome as quickly as possible. They can be controlled by shutting your eyes for a moment, which relieves the disorienting effect of the light rays. It can also be stopped by finding the bottom or any stable object. Of course, the simplest solution is to surface by using the anchor line, compass, bubbles, bottom, depth gauge, or buddy as references. Always use positive buoyancy when you surface.

DIRECTION CONTROL

Descending

Descending into dirty, dark water the first time can cause anxiety among even the most experienced divers. (See figure 5-10.) Knowing the area prior to diving is an important aspect of being comfortable. Descending through turbid water can be disconcerting in several ways. You must use all your senses to determine how fast you are descending, how deep you are, and to generally keep the descent in perspective. It requires a keen sense of your surroundings.

Fig. 5-10 Limited Visibility

Light from the surface dims quite rapidly as you begin to descend. In most cases, the temperature also changes. The change in temperature may not be very extreme, depending on the time of year and the area. The increase in pressure in your ears and around your mask also indicates descent. Even your exhalations sound different. Of course, you can always tell you are descending by watching your depth gauge. A small weighted object hung from a strap and bubbles can also indicate up-and-down directions.

Another way to eliminate the question of "which way is up," is by using ascent and descent lines. You do not necessarily need them when diving very close to shore or on shallow reefs, and you should not use them if there is a possibility of getting them entangled with yourself or equipment. However, they are recommended for low visibility diving in deeper water and from boats.

You can control the rate of descent by being aware of how quickly your senses change, and by controlling buoyancy. Start by having neutral buoyancy on the surface and by releasing air from your buoyancy control device until descent begins. To descend slowly, you should add small amounts of air to the buoyancy control device. By remaining calm and relaxed and not descending to depths that cause discomfort, you can descend with few, if any problems.

Horizontal Direction Control

The best, and quite often the *only* sure way to maintain horizontal direction control on the bottom, is with a compass. This is particularly true in fresh waters where the bottom may be mud or plain sand with no distinguishing characteristics. You must be skilled in compass use and have absolute confidence in your ability to navigate with this instrument when you dive in turbid water. Your senses occasionally indicate that you should proceed in a direction when the compass says otherwise. It takes real discipline to believe in and depend on the compass.

Natural Direction Finders

In addition to the compass and dive plan, you must have a well-tuned sense of natural direction, and knowledge of natural direction finders. There are several methods to help you locate position without a compass.

1. Follow a ledge for a predetermined time, then turn around and follow it back.
2. Remember bottom features, such as rocks, coral, ravines, or ledges.
3. Move along a slope to the left, and return with the slope on the right.
4. Be aware of the shape of the bottom and know that ripples on the bottom generally run parallel to the shore. (See figure 5-11.)
5. Determine the relative direction of the sun or the moon if the extent of turbidity allows it.
6. Remember the direction of current.
7. Use large plant growth, such as kelp, to observe current and depth.
8. Be aware of sudden depth changes.

Fig. 5-11 Ripples on Bottom

Again, a general sense of the surroundings is a must. Make a mental note of everything you see so you can remember them in the future. In fresh water, it is very important to stay off the bottom, as shown in figure 5-12, to avoid disturbing the silt in case you must return the same way. If you do find yourself grabbing onto objects on the bottom, wear heavy gloves so you will not be cut on sharp objects, such as broken glass or sharp metal. Also, you should position one hand in front of you and one under your chest as you swim. This technique chases away any animals that hide on the bottom. Always carry a dive knife, as entanglements on fishing lines or other lines and ropes can be a problem.

Fig. 5-12 Swimming Above Bottom

Ascending

Before proceeding for the surface, you should establish neutral buoyancy, simply to assure that you *will* ascend. It is nearly impossible to tell if you are rising except by subtle physical changes in the body and in the surrounding water. Consequently, you must be keenly aware of the physical changes. Pay attention to any increase in light and warmth in the water. As the buoyancy control device begins to inflate, you ascend more rapidly.

Release the air in the buoyancy control device to a slightly buoyant level and ascend at the same approximate rate as the smallest bubbles. Once you begin to ascend in turbid water, you should continue all the way to the surface. Remember to keep one hand overhead so you will avoid hitting any obstructions above you.

DIVE PLANNING

There are several ingredients to a good dive plan. One of the major ones is buddy responsibility. This begins with thoroughly knowing your buddy's gear as well as your own, including the location of buckles and the position of the octopus regulator; the tank size; and your buddy's general diving ability, including how well he or she can handle stress.

Because you must pay attention to so many things while diving in turbid water, stress becomes more of a possibility. You need to develop conditioned

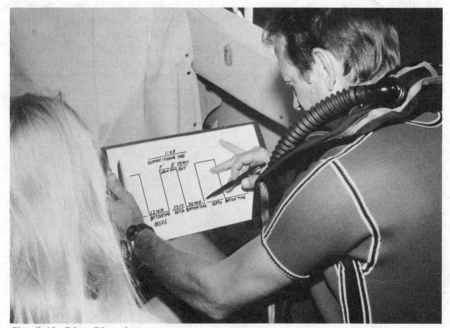

Fig. 5-13 Dive Planning

Fig. 5-14 Technique for Staying Together

responses so you can deal with potentially stressful situations. There is little room for mistakes. This means you must know *before* diving exactly what you are going to do. Prior to any dive, but especially in turbid water, carefully plan your dive, as shown in figure 5-13. Plan your diving time based on your air consumption rate at the intended depths so you return with one-third of the air in your tank. Enter all pertinent data in your logbook before entering the water and get in the habit of doing the dive as well as possible. Avoiding problems under stress involves proper training and repetition of good habits.

Buddy Techniques

When you dive in limited visibility conditions, it is necessary to frequently check with your buddy. You should always be able to see your buddy and be within reach. If you find it hard to stay together, hold hands, hold your buddy's tank harness, or use a buddy line. (See figure 5-14.) However, you and your buddy must agree before the dive on what procedure to use if you become separated. In this situation, you should immediately attempt to locate your buddy. Stop and listen for breathing sounds or other signals your buddy might attempt to make. If location has not been made after one minute, rejoin on the surface. If you still have not found each other, look for bubbles and initiate a search at once.

Activities in Turbid Water

Virtually every activity that can be done in clear water can be done in limited visibility. Hobbies, such as photography, for example, require that you take closeups, instead of panoramic shots. (See figure 5-15.) Hunters must be doubly alert and explorers can concentrate on small areas. Collecting artifacts is another good activity for turbid water. The closer range of vision lets you see objects you might otherwise miss.

WATER AT NIGHT

The underwater world at night is truly special. After sunset, both fresh water and salt water are usually calmer and more serene than during the day. Yet, this environment is exciting because the darkness gives

Fig. 5-15 Closeup Photography

you a narrowed field of vision; it takes longer than normal to inspect each nook and cranny. You can experience new sensations and life forms. Your artificial light illuminates brilliant colors, and objects appear even nearer and larger than they do during the day.

LIFE FORMS

Many different species of animals are active at night. This is the best time for them to feed without being threatened by their natural enemies. Since the darkness provides them with a protective cloak, these nocturnal creatures tend to be tame. Some allow you to touch them; whereas during the day, you are fortunate to even see them. (See figure 5-16.) Many of these

Fig. 5-16 Tame Night Creatures

creatures are drawn to your underwater light like magnets. The hypnotic effect of the light also makes them easy to touch.

One unique characteristic of the water at night is *bioluminescence*, the emission of light from millions of tiny planktonic organisms that inhabit the water. When this phenomenon occurs, any movement in the water creates a blue-green glow. Creatures, including humans, swim along and you can witness their phosphorescent trails. When you turn off your light, your own body even glows in the dark.

NIGHT DIVING

While night diving is undoubtedly quite spectacular, it also contains an element of danger. To minimize that danger, it is essential to not dive in an area that is completely unfamiliar to you. Always dive in an area either you or your buddy has seen In the daytlme. Ideally, the area you choose for nlght diving should have easy access, be rather shallow, and have a good reef formation. Heavy surf, offshore reefs, and thick kelp should be avoided at night. If you cannot dive from a boat, choose a night diving spot that protects you from surf, tidal changes, and other strong water movement. Bays and peninsulas are usually good for diving from the shore.

You also should be aware of other conditions. The water should be clear. Know what the visibility probability is. It is very unwise to dive in low visibility at night. Know what the bottom is like; whether it is rocky, sandy, or muddy. Determine the maximum depth you intend to go and do not exceed that limit.

You should be aware of the marine life you will probably see. While it is unlikely any harmful creatures will be in the vicinity, it is not impossible. Being aware of how they may react to divers and underwater lights can prepare you and help you avoid any possible confrontation. Make sure the dive is enjoyable by removing all undue stress and unnecessary hazards before you dive.

Night diving is safe when you take all the necessary precautions to eliminate errors. It is an activity for people who are capable in the water and confident of their ability. It is *not* an activity for people who are claustrophobic, who fear the dark, or who are at all unsure of their diving skills.

EQUIPMENT

Night diving requires that you have more thorough equipment knowledge than is needed in daytime limited visibility diving. You need enough good equipment to dive safely, in addition to proper gear preparation.

Equipment required for any dive, and which is especially important at night, begins with the buoyancy control device. Neutral buoyancy control is absolutely essential at night, particularly in fresh water, so you can stay off the bottom and avoid stirring it more than necessary. You should have a mechanical inflator on your buoyancy control device, as shown in figure 5-17, to ensure positive control without needing to use both hands to inflate it orally. An octopus regulator is an essential item.

You need to carry a whistle. If you and your buddy become separated on the surface or underwater, or if you lose your light

Fig. 5-17 Mechanical Inflator

source, the whistle can be used to reunite you. Search teams may also use whistles to locate lost divers. The diving knife is necessary for diving at night. It should be within your immediate reach, as well as being sharp, so you can quickly free yourself of any lines or rope. Gloves are as much a requirement for night diving as they are for diving in turbid water. They protect you from cutting yourself on sharp objects which cannot be seen at night.

The compass is an essential piece of safety equipment for night diving as well as diving in turbid water during the day. It points the way back to the entry point, be it on the boat or on the shore.

EQUIPMENT PREPARATION

Go over all your gear and make sure everything is correctly adjusted before leaving for the dive site. It is difficult to dress and adjust your equipment in the dark. Poorly adjusted gear also creates unnecessary stress that can result in problems. Specifically, adjust your fins so they fit over the wet suit boots and secure the straps. Make sure your weight belt has exactly the right amount of weight and that the weights are properly located and secured. Check all straps on every piece of equipment and make sure they are the right length and are set exactly to the correct size. In short, be sure everything about your equipment is right and know where everything is located.

UNDERWATER LIGHTS

The most essential additional piece of equipment for night diving is obviously the underwater light. Before selecting a light, you must first know how you intend to use it. Lights range from small penlight battery lights, as shown in figure 5-18, small chemical glow lights and strobe lights, as shown in figure 5-19, to large lights which are powered by motorcycle batteries, as shown in figure 5-20. The uses for these lights vary; it is not inconceivable that you may want a combination of lights for any given dive to assure safety.

Fig. 5-18 Penlight Battery Light

Fig. 5-19 Small Underwater Lights

The small penlite battery lights are generally used as backup or safety lights or to carry during daytime for casual observation under rocks or into tight places. Another safety light is the chemical light. It is preferred to the strobe light because it provides a constant visible light, which will glow for several hours. You should carry it on your body so your location is obvious to your buddy.

Fig. 5-20 Large Underwater Light

The large multi-cell flashlights, as shown in figure 5-21, are fine for occasional night diving. Rechargeable lights, as shown in figure 5-22, are powered by a nickel-cadmium battery pack which may be recharged by plugging it into a wall socket. They have up to 100,000 or more candlepower and are certainly the best general light for night diving. The brightest lights made for night

Fig. 5-21 Multi-Cell Flashlight

diving are the very large lights. They also have the nickel-cadmium battery pack and may cast, in some cases, as much as 300,000 candlepower. (See figure 5-23.) These are primarily for the serious night or cave diver.

There are even larger lights available, which utilize motorcycle or similar batteries and illuminate a greater area than the lights previously mentioned. These lights, however, are primarly used for very clear water. They also are expensive and are somewhat awkward to use, except for very capable divers.

When you find the light suitable for your needs, it is essential to check several other features.

1. Check the light output and beam angle in a darkened room. You need narrower beams for more penetration of light and wider beams for closeup work.

Fig. 5-22 Rechargeable Lights   Fig. 5-23 Large Underwater Light

2. The case surrounding the light itself should be durable.
3. The "O" ring seal must be positive and stable.
4. You should be able to hold and operate the light in one hand while you are wearing gloves.
5. The switch should have a lock to prevent the light from accidentally turning on when not in use.
6. Check to see how long the light takes to completely recharge.
7. The light should have a manufacturer's guarantee.

Light Preparation

In preparing your light for a night dive, first make sure the batteries are completely charged, if they are of the rechargeable type, or that the light has new batteries. Next, you should clean and lubricate it. This begins with cleaning the "O" rings and making sure they are free of defects and have been properly relubricated. (See figure 5-24.) Next clean the "O" ring lands and see if there is a proper seat. Then clean and check the contacts on the light, as shown in figure 5-25, and check for good electrical continuity. Reseal the light to make sure it is leakproof.

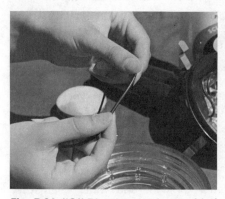 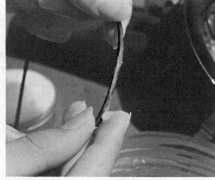

Fig. 5-24 "O" Ring Inspection and Lubrication

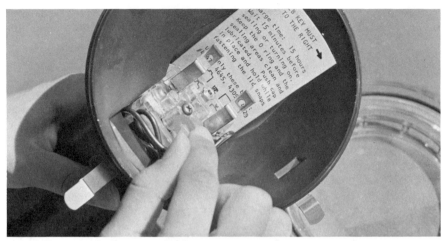

Fig. 5-25 Inspection of Contacts on Light

Once you have reassembled the light and are sure it is working properly, check the lanyard. The light is attached to the wrist by the lanyard so you cannot lose the light if you drop it. It should be adjustable and secure. An excellent lanyard is the shock absorber used on spearguns, as shown in figure 5-26. It is rubber with nylon loops on both ends. When these loops are joined, the lanyard is formed. When attached to the light, the loops make the lanyard adjustable and stretchy so the whole device is not only secure, but comfortable as well.

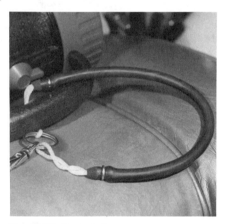

Fig. 5-26 Lanyard

Using the Underwater Light

The underwater light is simple to use. Unlike limited visibility diving in the daytime, you can point the light directly at the object you want to illuminate. You and your buddy should designate a system of signalling with lights. For example, to gain your buddy's attention, you may want to flash the light back and forth or turn the light on and off. However, you should never shine the light in your buddy's eyes, you should always aim for the body.

For safety purposes, you and your buddy should each have two lights and under no conditions should either one of you dive without a light. If one light floods or burns out, as occasionally happens, the dive should be terminated. With both of you having a second light as a backup, you are left with three lights should one burn out. This should give you a large enough safety margin to continue the dive.

If in an extreme case where all lights should be lost, hold hands with your buddy and establish positive buoyancy before leaving the bottom. Monitor your ascent rate and carefully ascend to the surface.

DIRECTIONAL CONTROL
Entering

When diving from shore, it is essential to have a light at your entry point, as shown in figure 5-27. This light not only helps you on entry, it also is a landmark to swim toward on your return. You may want to use permanent lights that you know will still be on when you end the dive, such as street lights. You may want to align these with auxiliary lights to show which direction to exit. Auxiliary lights include flashers, strobe lights, certain types of lanterns or roadside barricade flashers. Make sure any flashing lights you use are permitted on the beach. (See figure 5-28.)

Fig. 5-27 Lights at Entry Point

Fig. 5-28 Types of Entry Lights

The best type of auxiliary light to use is one that lights a wide area. This makes both the entry and the exit considerably safer and gives a constant shore beacon you can see if you need to surface for orientaton. When you use auxiliary lights, it is wise to have someone there to guard your light, especially if it is your only means of orienting yourself after the dive.

Prior to entering the water, again check your buddy's gear as well as your own. Agree once again on your dive plan, and take a compass reading in the direction you want to go. Then enter together and descend together or at least until you can see each other. Do not begin the actual dive until you have joined and are prepared to move on the bottom.

When diving from a boat at night, use the normal entry, but try to enter as quietly as possible to avoid disturbing the aquatic life. This type of entry is also much safer than plunging into dark water where there may be hidden obstacles.

Underwater Direction Control

You and your buddy should move along the bottom to the dive site, as opposed to moving on the surface. This naturally depends on conditions and the nature of the dive. However, a general rule is to keep the dive within a reasonably limited distance from your entry point. By following this rule, you will find that moving along the bottom to the actual dive site is preferable.

As previously mentioned, there is an interesting phenomenon that takes place at night when you are away from shore or underwater. The limits of visibility do not allow you to see a wide enough area for geograhic orientation, so it becomes nearly impossible to tell direction without moving directly along a coral head, ledge, or the bottom slope. On a flat, muddy bottom, it becomes virtually impossible to tell where you are and what direction you are going. For these reasons, you should use the compass.

Direction control is much easier if you have a surface float with a light, ascent/descent line, diving flag, and anchor. You use the light as a reference for ascending and descending.

Exiting

With the light at the entry point illuminating enough of the area, you can expect a safe exit. Use the normal procedure for exiting, but be particularly alert for hidden hazards below the surface at the exit point, as shown in figure 5-29. Pick a safe exit point where you can avoid areas of sharp coral, beds of sea urchins, sharp rocks, or other hazards.

DIVE PLANNING

A great deal has been said about the value of a dive plan. It is a point that can hardly be stressed enough, particularly for night diving. It is important

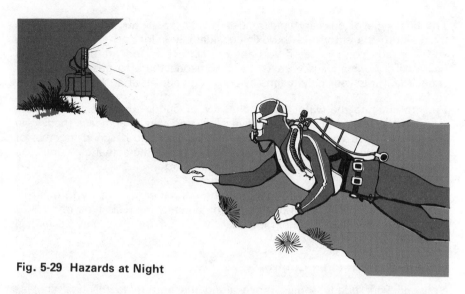

Fig. 5-29 Hazards at Night

that you follow an exact procedure because the continuity of the plan establishes the highest probability of safety.

Buddy Techniques

The buddy techniques for diving in turbid water and at night are generally the same. While diving, you must monitor your buddy's attitude. Be certain your buddy is comfortable, is moving smoothly and in a relaxed way, and is under control. Remember, the greatest potential for trouble is accidental separation.

Should separation occur, the procedure is much the same as for any limited visibility situation. Both you and your buddy should make two quick revolutions and attempt to rejoin. Look for your buddy's light and, at the same time, shine your light directly outward so it might cast its glare on your diving partner. (See figure 5-30.) If there is no contact after 30 seconds, go directly to the surface and rejoin. Should your buddy fail to come to the surface within 30 seconds, wait no more than another 30 seconds while looking for bubbles, and then immediately initiate a search.

Night Diving Activities

Most any underwater activity that can be enjoyed during the day can also be pleasant at night. But there are some particularly outstanding activities. One of those is photography. During the daytime when lights are unnecessary, the eye perceives color depending on the depth of the dive. However, at night, the sun is replaced by the artificial light which brings out those special and spectacular colors, which simply do not show up during the day. Of course, there is the new dimension of the additional creatures that appear at night. This also makes the night an excellent time for hunting and shell collecting.

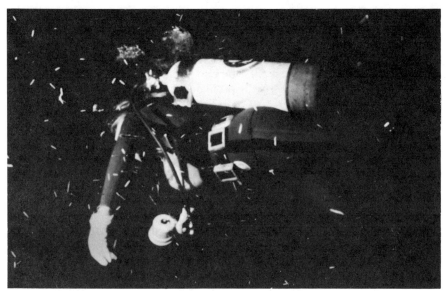

Fig. 5-30 Buddy Search

There are very few things that can compare with taking your own food and preparing it yourself. The night provides a false shelter for creatures, such as lobsters and crabs, as shown in figure 5-31, and for some of the more desirable shellfish. They come out of hiding, making them easier to locate and to capture than in the daytime. Night also provides an excellent opportunity for you to study these shy and interesting creatures and for exploration. Be sure to check on local fish and game laws. Taking some forms of shellfish, and in some cases, spearfishing, are illegal activities at night.

Fig. 5-31 Lobster and Crab

As you continue limited visibility diving, you may find that when you dive in clear water, your navigation skills, buoyancy control methods, and buddy system techniques, among others, have improved. You may also discover an increased sensitivity to your surroundings. By following these guidelines for diving in turbid water and at night, you can be in control of each dive, which enables you to routinely deal with problems and continue with your main objective — to enjoy the dive.

PART VI
diver stress

introduction

The psychology of diving deals mainly with diver stress. Stress is defined as "a physical, chemical, or emotional factor that causes bodily or mental tension." Stress can be any stimulus that disturbs or interferes with the normal psychological state. Most of the stress covered here is that which detracts from diving safety.

Scuba diving has a blend of both the physical and mental, as well as having definite social aspects. Diving is an enjoyable, interesting adventure.

There is a great psychological value to diving that is often overlooked, that is, to get away from the negative stresses or pressures of everyday life. Diving is beneficial because it is a demanding and rewarding activity. Other psychological attributes of diving include:

1. Feeling of weightlessness underwater
2. Personal ego satisfaction or inner feelings of self identity
3. Challenge of underwater activities
4. Freedom of the underwater world
5. Thrill of exploration, discovering new places, or seeing what few people, if any, have seen before
6. Excitement caused by an element of risk

The reasons people dive also include the social aspects of interacting with others who share the common interest in diving and gaining satisfaction from helping or teaching others. The very special interpersonal relationship of the buddy pair is not often shared in other human activities. After diving for some time, you can gain a feeling of oneness with yourself, your buddy, and the environment. After the dive, there is a feeling of well-being that is hard to describe to non-divers.

causes. effects. avoiding and dealing with stress. and loss of control

Sport diving is a demanding, yet rewarding adventure, and for many people, it may be their ultimate adventure. (See figure 6-1.) Diving can be the very essence of those activities that add joy to your life. Yet, with all this, diving can also subject you to stress. To be a safe diver, you need to understand the chain of events leading to stress; what the outcome of stress may be, if controlled; and what may happen if stress is not dealt with — usually an accident. The central idea is not to allow stress to develop, but if it does develop in either you or your buddy during a dive, you should understand how to control it.

Fig. 6-1 Clearest Water for Diving

CAUSES AND EFFECTS
OF DIVER STRESS

There are several physical and mental causes of diver stress. Some of these causes, in turn, can be brought about by different actions, for example, overloading can develop from working too long or too hard underwater. In addition, it is difficult to isolate each cause as the only factor leading to stress, for several of these usually combine to create significant stress.

Individual psychological makeup and life experience also need to be considered when studying the causes and effects of diver stress. What puts one diver into a serious state of stress may leave another diver totally unconcerned and in full control of the situation.

These causes and effects are not meant to discourage you from diving, but they are realistic and they may happen. To be a competent advanced sport diver, you should become very familiar with them so you will be able to avoid them or deal with the stress evolving from them.

PHYSICAL CAUSES

Major physical causes of diver stress include: pre-dive stress, poor physical fitness, distance, fatigue, overloading, environmental conditions, equipment difficulties, air supply and ascent difficulties, and problems with buoyancy. Each of these must be viewed in relation to each other and to the mental aspects of stress when studying the effects.

Pre-Dive Stress

The time before any dive is just as important as the dive itself. The pre-dive begins when you decide to make a dive, be it one day, or two months in advance. How you feel about diving during this time sets the mood for the actual dive. If you are confident this dive will be relaxing and pleasurable, that is what you will most likely experience. On the other hand, if you are apprehensive, you will probably be a target for diver stress.

The time element is a big factor in producing pre-dive stress. If your diving companions are already suited up and ready to jump in the water while you are struggling with the wet suit zipper or searching for your depth gauge, stress could obviously occur. A stressful state can, in turn, cause you to overlook crucial things, such as checking your regulator, or you may overlook a necessary piece of equipment in your rush to plunge into the water.

Poor Physical Fitness

Diving requires good physical fitness. If you are not in good shape, even the simplest movements or skills may cause you to go beyond your physical capabilities, which may bring on stress. (See figure 6-2.) Poor physical fitness also includes any significant problem which affects respiration, circulation, consciousness, ability to equalize pressure, or judgment. Examples of these are:

1. Heart trouble
2. Respiratory impairment
3. Epilepsy
4. Regular medication to control a serious condition
5. Ear and sinus trouble
6. Recent serious operation
7. Injury or illness

Fig. 6-2 Poor Diver Fitness

Certain temporary conditions or activities, such as colds, influenza, excessive drinking, use of drugs, and fatigue, can also cause stress.

Some conditions deserve special consideration when related to diving. A physical handicap does not necessarily prohibit diving, provided the diver with the handicap can still relate to and effectively rescue the buddy diver, should the need arise. Age plays a role in diving; as you get older, you may need to be more conservative in your range of diving activities. But of even more importance is your level of fitness at *any* age.

Recent research indicates that women who are pregnant should be very conservative about scuba diving. The key issue is not the exercise of diving, but the physiological changes that occur under pressure, particularly as related to decompression sickness. This affects both the mother and, more importantly, the fetus. Women should do only shallow diving during pregnancy.

Smoking deserves special consideration, as it significantly detracts from personal fitness. This is of particular concern during diving where the respiratory system and gases under pressure are of extreme importance. If at all possible, divers should not smoke or decrease their smoking as much as possible. Smoking should be eliminated immediately before and after the dive. Smokers who have recovered from a cold within the last two weeks have a greater risk of embolism. Flem pockets may trap air when ascending.

Fatigue

Fatigue and poor physical fitness are interrelated, however, stress from fatigue can develop from several other activities. Staying in the water too long, as shown in figure 6-3, using equipment improperly, and lacking the proper equipment, can cause you to tire quickly. Fatigue can also be caused by overloading. Fatigue limits your ability to think before you notice any other signs. This adds greatly to stress.

Fig. 6-3 Exceeding Time Limit

Overloading

Overloading, like fatigue, can also be caused by the amount of time spent underwater, the distance you have to swim at a certain point during the dive, or an excessive amount of work required within a given time period. The work may encompass swimming, breathing, snorkeling, making a rescue, strenuous activity, or lack of buoyancy control. Having a great distance to swim or trying to do it too fast could cause overloading. Trying to make a rescue too rapidly is another example. All of these add to the stress level.

Environment

Dangerous or suddenly changing environmental conditions obviously can be major physical factors contributing to diver stress. Surf may be overwhelming, as shown in figure 6-4; caves may seem to have no exit point; unnoticed currents may affect your compass course; or some equipment may freeze while ice diving. Diving in cold water and at great depths can cause additional stress.

Fig. 6-4 Extreme Surf Conditions

Your stress level increases as the range of visibility, due to dirty or turbid water, night diving, or deep diving, decreases. Poor visibility also makes proper underwater orientation difficult; adding even more to stress.

Certain situations which are confining or restricting to bodily movement can cause stress. Examples of these may be entanglement in kelp, weeds, lines, or nets. (See figure 6-5.) Diving in caves, wrecks, or under ice may also contribute to the stress level. Diving equipment, such as a wet suit or buoyancy control device, can cause restrictions that add to stress.

Fig. 6-5 Entanglement in Kelp

Fig. 6-6 Physical Threat

Direct physical threats, of course, can impair your ability to cope. Some of these include animals that bite, such as moray eels, barracudas (see figure 6-6), and sharks. Boat propellers, boats immediately overhead when you are ascending, and spearguns are other direct physical threats. Other things already mentioned that may be considered threats are entangling sea weeds and dangerous water conditions, such as surf or current. Each of these is a possible threat, but most often the danger from them is grossly exaggerated.

Equipment Difficulties

If you are not completely familiar or comfortable with the diving equipment you use on a dive, stress could possibly result, especially when combined with any of the preceding causes of stress. A rental buoyancy control device could have an inflation device you are not used to or you may not have balanced the weights on your weight belt before entering the water. Any number of similar examples can cause stress. Also, if you have not properly maintained your equipment, problems, such as a leaking buoyancy control device or malfunctioning regulator, could lead to stress while you are diving.

Another stress factor to be aware of is the lack of needed equipment. If you look down at your wrist to check your time limit for a certain depth and your watch is missing, stress could very well develop. Remember that the primary problem is not the equipment itself, but what you do or forget to do with the equipment.

Air Supply and Ascents

A major cause of stress and resulting accidents is the "running out of air" situation with uncontrolled ascents. In most cases, a diver is actually just low on air (100 to 500 psi), so these cannot really be considered "out-of-air" situations. An instinctive response to running low on air is to head for the surface, and this, of course, is inappropriate if precautions against air embolism and decompression sickness are not taken. The prevention of stress in these situations will be discussed later.

Buoyancy Control Problems

Problems of stress associated with buoyancy happen when you do not have or use a buoyancy control device, if the buoyancy control device is not functioning, or if you are overweighted. Records of fatal diving accidents show that few people inflated their own buoyancy compensators or ditched their weights.

Drag, or resistance to movement in the water adds to the work of swimming. Buoyancy control equipment, when inflated, can add greatly to drag. Just moving in the water while you are wearing equipment requires that you overcome water resistance. This, coupled with concern about the distance to the surface or to your buddy, contributes to stress.

MENTAL CAUSES

Major mental causes of diver stress include: cultural views, ego threat, buddy system failure, lack of training, plus human error and mishaps. Again, these causes are very much tied in with the physical causes of stress, as well as being interrelated among themselves.

Cultural Views

Society's biased views may create a negative reaction in certain groups of people. These people believe they must prove they are as good or capable as other people. Because of this, stress on the *mental* level may develop when these particular groups desire to dive. For example, women are allegedly subordinate to men; certain racial and minority groups are supposedly not as capable in aquatics as other groups; older people are allegedly not as fit as younger people; and children, it is assumed, lack good judgment.

All these persons can be at a disadvantage in any recreational activity that involves stress. These cultural value judgments, of course, are not true, because you, as a diver, can perform activities based on your own merit and ability.

Ego Threat

Another mental cause of diver stress is ego threat. Your ego may be threatened when you must retreat from a situation that is too much for you to handle. If you are performing a certain underwater activity due to peer pressure or to prove to yourself it can be done, giving up can certainly affect your pride and bring on stress. It takes more maturity and a strong ego to admit you cannot do a difficult task, than to continue despite the risk of a diving accident.

Failure in many different areas, mainly mental, contributes to stress. Some of these include failing to enjoy the dive, to get some game while spearfishing, to make a rescue, to gain personal control, or to stay oriented underwater.

Buddy System Failure

When you lose contact with your buddy underwater, as shown in figure 6-7, or when you dive alone, the chances of a stressful situation developing increases. You do not have the security of knowing someone is there to help you if a problem occurs. While diving alone does not directly harm you, being alone when something goes wrong makes it difficult or sometimes impossible to safely deal with the situation.

Fig. 6-7 Loss of Buddy Contact

Lack of Training

Stress from lack of training may develop because of four different reasons. Divers are uncertified and untrained; dives are made without specialty training for cave, ice, wreck, or deep diving; diving is done with new or advanced equipment without specialized instruction; or diving is not done for many years and then done without any "refresher" training.

Scuba diving is complex and demanding, yet people still try it without proper training or supervision. The chances for stress and accidents are higher in untrained and uncertified divers than in those who are trained and certified, not only because they are not trained in basic fundamentals of diving, but also because they have not been shown how to recognize and deal with stress.

Human Error and Mishaps

Human error and mishaps are two additional causes of stress. Poor judgment includes mistakes made before or during the dive, which, by themselves, have been mentioned as sources of stress. These may be equipment misuse, lack of equipment maintenance, or diving with incomplete equipment; diving beyond the limits of fitness or environmental conditions; using drugs before the dive; and running out of air during the dive. These errors lead to or become mishaps, but in addition, even good equipment can malfunction, and environmental conditions can change or be unexpected. Any one, or several, of these causes of stress may come together or be caused by a human error, leading to a mishap that is a source of even more stress.

OVERALL EFFECTS OF STRESS

The overall physical effects of stress which can be observed in a diver include:

1. Muscle tension (white knuckles)
2. Wide-eyed look (See figure 6-8.)
3. Hyperventilation
4. Rapid, jerking movements
5. Fixation or repetitive behavior

In addition, many changes are happening inside the person as a reaction to stress. These cannot be observed easily by divers in the water. They include:

1. Chemical changes
2. Heart rate changes
3. Blood pressure changes
4. Increased perspiration
5. Decreased digestion

Fig. 6-8 Effect of Stress

Mental changes caused by stress that another diver can observe in the water include irritability, unexpected or unusual behavior, inappropriate responses, mental narrowing or fixation, inability to recall or use the correct action, loss of new skills, and narrowing visual focus increased by the tunnel vision effect of the mask.

All these effects of diver stress lead to additional, or cumulative, human errors, particularly in judgment. If prolonged enough, or if the diver does not gain control, stress can lead to accidents. Stress is not *always* a precedent for accidents, as something can happen quite unexpectedly and quickly underwater. However, surprise can create a sudden and high stress factor. The chain of events leading up to diving accidents is shown in figure 6-9.

AVOIDING STRESS

Anticipation of stress will help you avoid stress. Mentally performing a task beforehand usually reduces tension and stress when the task has to be done. Just as one cause of stress cannot be isolated as the *only* cause, one method of avoiding stress does not only deal with one particular type of stress. One technique may deal with many forms of stress, for example, gathering all the information possible about your dive and thoroughly planning it to eliminate the stresses of buddy separation, disorientation, dive termination or

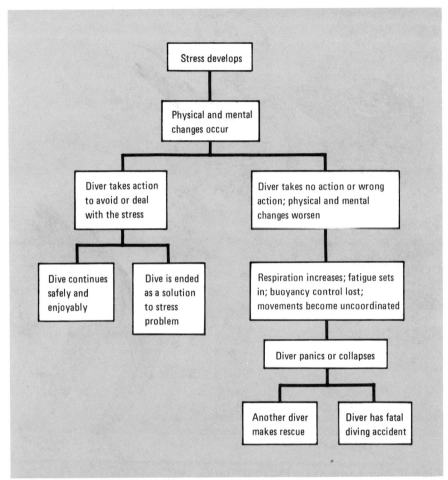

Fig. 6-9 Chain of Events

emergency ascents, to name a few. The objective is to eliminate surprise. You can avoid the harmful effects of stress by being physically fit, using proper and complete equipment, being trained and experienced, and planning each dive.

PHYSICAL FITNESS

There are several ways to improve and maintain physical fitness. First, a regular medical examination is important for health care in general, not just for diving. Medical examinations should be more frequent as you become older and the examinations should emphasize the requirements special to diving. Many diving organizations and textbooks have diving medical exam forms available.

Fig. 6-10 Requirements for Physical Fitness

To be physically fit, you should have adequate rest, have a well-balanced diet and exercise regularly, as shown in figure 6-10. These are all particularly important for divers. The amount of rest varies significantly with each person and the amount of activity performed. Maintaining a well-balanced diet of nutritious food and avoiding foods with low or no nutritional value is a problem for most people. It is not so much a problem of understanding what is best, as it is a problem of self-discipline.

Diving itself is an excellent way to stay in shape. So you can be more fit for diving, your exercise should parallel the demands of diving as much as possible. Activities similar to diving that increase circulation and respiration are good, such as: skin diving, snorkeling in a pool, swimming, bicycling, walking, jogging, running, and others that increase heart rate and breathing while utilizing leg movement.

Relaxation and recreation are important for good fitness. To be fit, you need to relieve the stress of everyday life. Again, diving is an excellent stress reliever. Other activities that contribute to relaxation and recreation also relieve stress and help you become a better diver.

Fitness immediately prior to diving is very important. There are some helpful hints that make diving more enjoyable by improving this short-term fitness. First, you should mentally want to make the dive and be physically well. Next, you should avoid alcohol and drugs as much as possible, particularly during the 12 hours immediately preceding the dive. If you use regular medication and understand its side effects, you should experience no problem, however, you should still check with your physician.

You should have a good night's sleep the night before the dive. You need to eat well both the night before and the morning of the dive. These meals should include easily digestible foods. Repeatedly equalizing the pressure in your ears the day and night before diving makes it easier to equalize during the dive.

Good mental and physical fitness is a lifestyle decision only you can make. It is not easy to be fit, but the reward of being fit not only improves your diving, it also increases your enjoyment of life by relieving stress.

EQUIPMENT USE

You can do a great deal to help avoid stress by using proper and complete equipment. Your regulator should be a well-maintained, single-hose, high-quality regulator, equipped with both a submersible pressure gauge and octopus regulator. A good buoyancy control device with a mechanical inflator connected to the scuba tank makes diving easier and, therefore, decreases stress.

Many causes of stress can be avoided by wearing a wet suit or dry suit. A wet suit jacket is recommended even in warm water. In colder water, wet suits should be thicker and more complete. In very cold water, you should use a dry or inflatable suit.

Your snorkel should be comfortable, with a large diameter and nothing to increase breathing resistance. A knife is a safety tool you should always carry to help deal with stressful situations. Information equipment, such as depth gauges, watches, and compasses, often needs to be used. New equipment, particularly new tanks and regulators or a new buoyancy control device, should be tested under controlled conditions in confined water, or under the supervision of an instructor before you use it in open water.

TRAINING AND EXPERIENCE

During your beginning diving course, you overlearned many skills and concepts to make you a safe diver. Overlearning means doing some skill or activity so often that you do it automatically during a difficulty. Now, you

Fig. 6-11 Additional Training

should continue your training in open water, with advanced, or specialty courses to continue that process. This is necessary to avoid stress and perform the proper response under difficult conditions. (See figure 6-11.)

Experience is vital to maintaining diving skills and being fit and relaxed during diving. This experience should be gained under controlled conditions within your diving ability.

DIVE PLANNING

It is important to plan your dive with your buddy prior to the actual dive. "Plan your dive — dive your plan" is a valuable concept, but it should be applied with common sense. The plan should not be so rigid that it takes the joy out of diving. Most of the plan can be verbal and it should be based on the least fit or experienced diver's limits.

During the dive, you and your buddy should make reasonable modifications to assure both safety and enjoyment. Also, an important aspect of dive planning is that either you or your buddy can, at anytime, decide not to dive, based on changing medical, physical, psychological, or environmental conditions.

The dive plan should include such items as:

1. Objective
2. Equipment
3. Environmental conditions
4. Diver fitness
5. Buddy system
6. General direction of dive
7. Exit and entry points

8. Planned depth
9. How changes will be made
10. Criteria for dive termination
11. Possible stress factors
12. Hand signals
13. Emergency procedures

DEALING WITH STRESS

Much of the material just presented covers anticipating stress. You can anticipate significant changes when you enter the water. (See figure 6-12.) You have little or no control over these changes, so you must learn to adapt to them. Your heart rate, blood pressure, respiration, and temperature all decrease. Your center of gravity moves and your body weight decreases to nearly zero. You are restricted by your wet suit, straps, and belts. The mask narrows your field of vision, while the range of visibility and color decreases. The unfamiliar surroundings and vertical dimension make it hard to orient yourself and you may feel apprehension of the unknown or unseen.

With all these changes, you need to pause, with your buddy, usually at the surface *and* at the bottom, breathe easily, and allow the body and mind to adjust to all these changes. When you feel ready to proceed, and your buddy gives the "OK" signal, start the dive in a slow, easy mannner. You should always function within the environment and not attempt to overcome it.

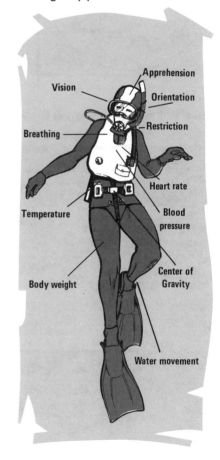

Fig. 6-12 Adaptation

BREATHING, MOVING, AND ORIENTATION

The techniques for all three of these skill areas are interrelated and cover the skills of swimming, snorkeling, buoyancy control, navigation, breathing, and ascents.

Breathing takes work; uses energy; increases stress; and becomes more difficult if you go deeper, or swim or work harder. The easiest way to breathe is

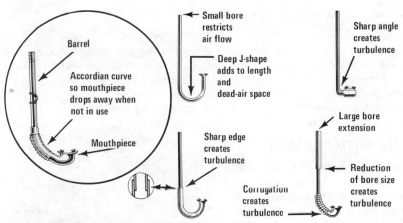

Fig. 6-13　Changes in Snorkel Design

Fig. 6-14　Underwater Compass Use

Fig. 6-15　Surface Use of Compass

through your mouth at the surface. The next easiest way is through the regulator and the least easiest is through the snorkel. The snorkel is necessary for surface swimming. The design has improved greatly, as shown in figure 6-13, but it still is the most difficult way to breathe. All divers need to carry and regularly use a snorkel, but there are excellent ways to avoid using it so often, thereby decreasing the work and stress of diving.

You should always use a compass for underwater navigation so you can arrive at your exit point without a long surface swim. (See figure 6-14.) When you ascend and are at the surface, the buoyancy control device can be comfortably inflated. Occasionally you can swim on your back, as shown in figure 6-15, breathing easily and occasionally checking the direction by looking over your shoulder, or better yet, using the compass to navigate a reciprocal course. Do not swim on your back in a rough water situation. When surface conditions are too rough for snorkeling, use the regulator. This is one reason for saving that last 500 psi of air.

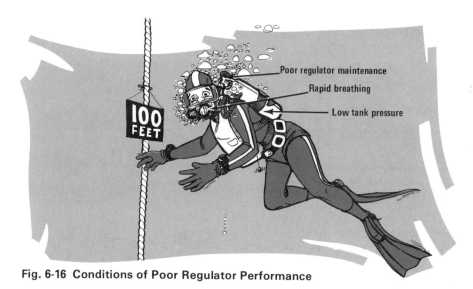

Fig. 6-16 Conditions of Poor Regulator Performance

Regulators are high-quality pieces of equipment, but it is possible to demand too much air from them, if you are not careful. Regulators perform at less than design capacity, when the tank pressure is 500 psi or less, at a depth of 100 feet or more, when you have a rapid breathing rate, or when the regulator is poorly maintained. (See figure 6-16.) To reduce the work and stress of diving, select the best single-hose regulator possible and have it professionally serviced every year. In addition, avoid deep diving, hold 500 psi in reserve, and breathe in a slow, deep, relaxed manner.

Swimming with fins is work and this may increase the stress level. You should use fins as efficiently as possible, with strong, slow kicks from the hips while you point your toes, as shown in figure 6-17. This reduces fatigue.

Fig. 6-17 Proper Fin Kick

Fig. 6-18 Mid-Water Buoyancy Control

Descend and ascend mainly with buoyancy control, as shown in figure 6-18, not by swimming. Neutral buoyancy aids movement when you are on the bottom. Hands and fins can be used to pull and push along the bottom. This bottom crawling technique, of course, depends on the nature of the bottom.

In a "low on air" or "out of air" situation, a normal ascent is the best option whenever possible. You should stop, breathe easy, be in control, and then swim to the surface. The next option is to ascend, using your buddy's octopus regulator, provided the buddy is closer than the surface or there is an obstruction to the surface (ice, cave, wreck, or heavy kelp).

The third option is the emergency swimming ascent performed as closely to a normal ascent as possible. This includes looking up, regulator in mouth, swimming a bit faster, exhaling more and inhaling less to keep lungs at as near normal volume as possible. The fourth option is a buoyant ascent done by ditching weights and/or inflating the buoyancy control device. This is done like an emergency swimming ascent, but it is faster.

As a last resort, and when no other option is available, use the buddy breathing ascent, as shown in figure 6-19. Out-of-air ascents will be rare if

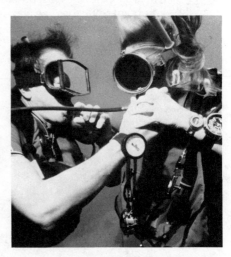

Fig. 6-19 Buddy Breathing Ascent

you use submersible pressure gauges, reserves, octopus regulators, the buddy system, relaxed breathing, dive planning, good fitness, buoyancy control, and if you dive within your limitations.

By using and carrying only the necessary equipment, keeping your equipment as simple and streamlined as possible, and swimming slowly while staying completely underwater, you can decrease the drag created by equipment, especially the buoyancy control device. (Note figure 6-20.) You should weight yourself for the most common or shallowest depth of the dive and maintain neutral or slightly negative buoyancy with as little air as possible in the buoyancy control device.

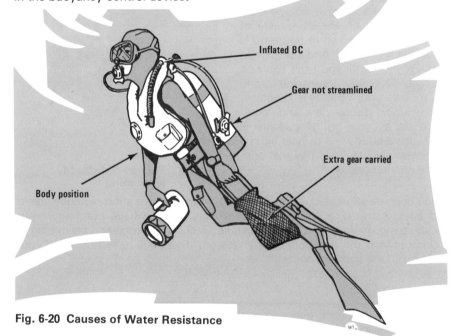

Inflated BC

Gear not streamlined

Extra gear carried

Body position

Fig. 6-20 Causes of Water Resistance

Orientation is extremely important in the three-dimensional underwater world. To deal with and avoid stress, follow the bottom contour or an anchor line, swim a compass course, watch your bubbles or your buddy, use buoyancy, or check your depth gauge. Each, or better, *several* of these methods can give you a sense of location and orientation in the watery inner space. This, in turn, decreases the stress level.

ENVIRONMENTAL CONDITIONS

Surface chop, surge, surf, current, poor visibility, and cold water cannot be changed. These conditions need special training, additions or modifications to equipment, controlled and supervised diving situations, buddy diving, and a complete understanding of diver stress. Proper planning and techniques can help you deal with the environment.

BUDDY DIVING

The greatest value of buddy diving is the increased enjoyment of the dive. The buddy arrangement becomes a very special interpersonal relationship. It should be a sharing, supportive, and growing relationship.

In order to buddy dive more easily, select a buddy with common interests and abilities. Then plan the dive with common or compatible objectives. Right before the dive, check each other's equipment, and agree on emergency procedures and hand signals.

Once in the water, dive side-by-side, always staying on the same side of your buddy, as shown in figure 6-21. Agree on a direction and continue in that direction until you both agree to change. Go slowly, look around, and listen for your buddy's bubbles. Share your discoveries and communicate as you go. If visibility is poor, use a buddy line or hold hands. It is reassuring to have physical contact with your buddy.

Fig. 6-21 Side-by-Side Buddy Swimming

If you become separated, stop, look, and listen. Move a short distance ahead and back in the direction you were traveling. If you have not found your buddy, bang on your tank while ascending a short distance and swimming in a circle toward the side your buddy was on. If you still have not found your buddy, surface and look for bubbles.

LIMITATIONS

"Know your limits and dive within them" is an excellent concept, but it is quite difficult to put into practice. The situation is complex: there are two of you, each with different limits imposed by fitness, skill level, experience, equipment, environment and, of course, stress. These limits also change from day to day. On top of all this, you and your buddy should provide or hold back a "margin of safety," a reserve of energy to use in case the other should need help.

Sport dives should not test the limits of either you or your buddy. If you discover your limits by exceeding them in open water, you will be in a very unsafe situation. When either of you is cold, tired, getting low on air, not feeling well, or having difficulty, injured, uncomfortable, under undue stress, or not having a good time, you should leave the water — diving is no longer safe or enjoyable.

When the decision has been made to end the dive, do not rush to get out of the water. Rushing will increase stress and may lead to an accident during the swim back. First, stop, breathe easy, and check the situation; then proceed slowly and easily. Use your equipment skillfully to make the trip as easy as possible.

TREATING SYMPTOMS

If you or your buddy is experiencing physical or mental symptoms of stress, you need to break the chain of events, as shown previously in figure 6-9, or a diving accident could occur. People have a survival instinct that provides the drive often needed to escape difficult situations. But this survival instinct may cause you to make the wrong decision of rushing to the surface.

The symptoms of stress should be treated as soon as you recognize them. The crucial elements in dealing with stress when symptoms have appeared are: stop, breathe easy, think, and get control. (See figure 6-22.) Additional steps are:

1. Use your equipment to help.
2. Control your buoyancy.
3. Let your buddy help.
4. Maintain your orientation.
5. Solve the problem when you are under control.
6. Continue slowly in the easiest possible manner.

Fig. 6-22 Controlled Diver

The best place to solve a problem is on the bottom. If you are already on the surface, use positive buoyancy to help you. Maintaining control is the all-important aspect in dealing with diver stress. Loss of control leads to panic and accidents.

LOSS OF CONTROL

If you do not recognize the causes and effects of stress so you can avoid or deal with it, stress may lead to the total loss of control, which is panic. Panic is a sudden unreasoning fear that causes the diver to take inappropriate action in dealing with the situation. The causes and effects of panic and stress are the same. Panic can be thought of as an acute case of stress, with exaggeration on inappropriate behavior and errors in judgment.

Treatment for panic is the same as avoiding and dealing with stress, except that it may now be necessary for the diving buddy or another responsible diver to rescue the panicked diver. In this case, another person takes a risk to help someone who has allowed stress to go too far. You can prevent panic by watching for early physical and mental signs of stress in yourself and in your buddy.

Discipline your thinking to recognize and solve problems instead of worrying about them. You can develop self-control in your thinking behavior with training and practice. Concentration maintains self-discipline. Concentrate on those parts of the problem that are important and ignore the emotional consequences. In this way, you can effectively handle stress.

PART VII
diver rescue

introduction

Many of the reasons and methods for diver rescue come from studying the effects of diver stress. Understanding the causes of stress that may lead to accidents is a large part of diver rescue. Avoiding and dealing with stress are the very essence of accident prevention; this makes diver rescues unnecessary. Finally, panic, or the collapse of a diver's ability to continue functioning are the times when diver rescue becomes all-important.

rescue considerations. situations. procedures. and skills

The greatest value of mastering diver rescue is to you personally. The knowledge and skills of diver rescue make you a better, more confident and capable diver, able to help yourself, and avoid trouble. The intention of this material is not to make you a diving lifeguard or member of a search and recovery team, but to help you be a more responsible diver and buddy. Still, someday, your rescue skills may be used to help another diver other than your buddy, or even to help a non-diver.

RESCUE CONSIDERATIONS
ENVIRONMENT

The remarkably diverse, demanding, and interesting diving environment adds greatly to your enjoyment of diving; but, during a diving rescue, the environment may make the rescue more difficult.

Diving accidents often occur far from the shore or boat, in deep water, or in poor visibility. The water may be moving with surge, surf, surface chop, or currents. Caves, ice, wrecks, or kelp may restrict movement and coral or other aquatic growth may make it difficult to leave the water. The water may be cold, and, therefore, drain your energy. The accident could occur underwater or on the surface.

These diverse environmental conditions can usually be handled if you are trained and if you operate within reasonable limits. Difficult environmental conditions clearly show why you need a "margin of safety," a reserve of energy for rescues made at these times. The rescue procedures and skills detailed later provide ways to deal with these conditions.

COMPLICATIONS

You need to consider other possible complications during a rescue. The diver may have an injury or diving malady, such as air embolism, decompression sickness, a squeeze, wounds, or heart attack. Because of the three-dimensional nature of scuba diving, the diver could be upside down, twisted, or entangled. Cold and fatigue are also common problems. Cramps from cold water and/or the hard work of swimming add to complications. Stress leading to panic is, of course, a major complication. Another major

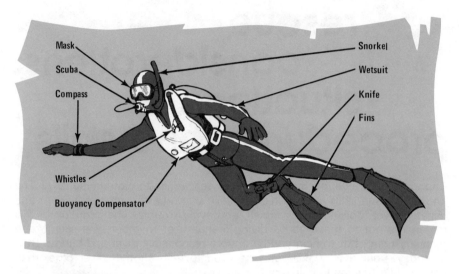

Fig. 7-1 Useful Equipment for Rescues

complication is the collapse into unconsciousness that can lead to cessation of breathing.

DIVING EQUIPMENT

Even though some diving equipment may be in the way or impose some limitation to movement during a rescue, equipment greatly enhances the ease and safety of diving rescues. (See figure 7-1.) Equipment makes diver rescues easier and safer than rescuing a swimmer.

The mask lets you see underwater and protects the face. Fins give you power, speed, and maneuverability to reach a victim or to get out of a tight situation yourself. Both the snorkel and scuba equipment offer alternate breathing methods. Protection and reserve buoyancy come from the wet suit. Buoyancy control equipment makes resting and artificial respiration at the surface reasonable possibilities. Surface floats add another dimension of ease and safety to diving and compasses can be used during diver rescue tows. Diver's knives can be used to cut entanglements or as all-purpose tools and, finally, you can use your whistle to call for help.

There are some additional equipment considerations to remember during diver rescues. Any breathing resistance due to diving equipment can add to the work of a diving rescue. You should use the easiest way to breathe in any particular situation. Remember, breathing through your mouth at the surface is the easiest possible way. Anything held in your hands can contribute to the difficulty or prevent the rescue. The buddy making the rescue should hold or leave behind game bags, spears, cameras, and so forth, as shown in figure 7-2. You may need to remove your gloves or mitts if they interfere with a rescue.

Fig. 7-2 Ditching Gear

It should be an automatic response to inflate the buoyancy control device, ditch the weight belt, or both, when positive buoyancy is necessary. Weight belts should be brightly colored with quick-release buckles. They should be ditched vertically and as far away from the body as possible, as shown in figure 7-3, to assure they will not snag on the diver's other equipment. The buoyancy control device should have a mechanical inflator for easy inflation during a rescue.

RESCUE SITUATIONS AND PROCEDURES

SELF RESCUE

Your first line of defense against diving difficulties should be prevention. When prevention has failed and you still have a problem, you should be prepared to deal with difficulties

Fig. 7-3 Ditching Weight Belt

yourself, that is, make a *self rescue*. This is by far the most important and most used form of rescue. Because self rescue is not dramatic and does not require outside help, it most often goes unnoticed. In addition, many everyday diving skills are self-help and self-rescue techniques. These include:

1. Buoyancy control, including resting on the surface
2. Emergency swimming and buoyant ascents
3. Survival swimming techniques, as shown in figure 7-4, including treading water, bobbing, floating, swimming in place, snorkel breathing, or drownproofing
4. Ditching the weight belt
5. Changing to alternate fin kicks when tired, such as flutter, scissors, dolphin, or frog kicks; or swimming on your back
6. Being able to take off, adjust, and replace dive gear in the water
7. Relieving leg cramps, as shown in figure 7-5, by stopping activity and holding the fin tip while straightening the leg or massaging it
8. Switching from one breathing method to another, as needed, such as snorkel, scuba, or with no equipment
9. Mask and regulator clearing

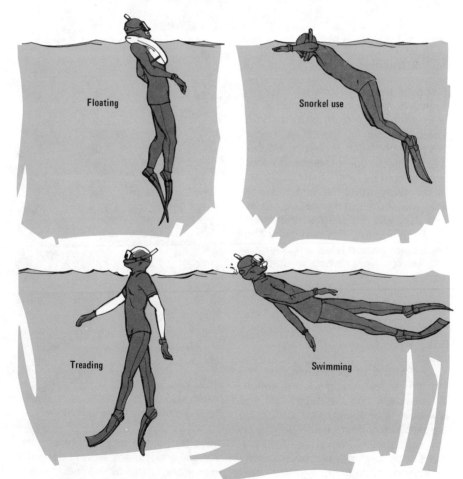

Floating

Snorkel use

Treading

Swimming

Fig. 7-4 Survival Swimming Techniques

Fig. 7-5 Releasing Leg Cramp

Much of your basic diver training taught you to take care of difficulties for yourself, but this certainly does *not* prevent your buddy from lending a helping hand. In fact, this is the best possible way to make a self rescue. When you handle a problem, such as replacing a fin that has slipped off, as shown in figure 7-6, your buddy can hold the game bag and hold onto you to steady you. Working together has the added advantage that both of you are aware of the problem.

Fig. 7-6. Buddy Helping During Self Rescue

BUDDY ASSIST

The *buddy assist* is a natural outgrowth of working together and of the relationship you and your buddy already have. It can be as simple as the reassuring touch of your hand on your buddy's arm or as extensive as towing your buddy all the way to shore. Quite often, the assist will be so natural that it seems to have no relation to diver rescue. Other times, it will be apparent to both you and your buddy that a situation could have turned into a serious diving accident if one of you had not assisted the other.

Again, during your diver training, you acquired many skills that may be used to help your buddy. These same skills are often used in the more serious situation of a buddy rescue.

1. Helping your buddy hold, remove, and replace gear
2. Inflating your buddy's buoyancy control device, as shown in figure 7-7
3. Towing your buddy
4 Ditching your buddy's equipment, particularly the weight belt
5. Helping your buddy who is entangled
6. Responding to your buddy's hand signals
7. Shared air octopus breathing
8. Buddy breathing

In the normal course of diving activities, you and your buddy should use and practice these skills. This makes these skills a natural and comfortable part of diving. When your buddy needs assistance, approach him or her so you can

Fig. 7-7 Inflating Buddy's Buoyancy Control Equipment

Fig. 7-8 Approaching Buddy for Rescue

be seen, as shown in figure 7-8, and make physical contact. The touch of your hand reassures your buddy. Both of you should then stop, breathe easy, think, communicate, and proceed when you are both in control.

Proceed slowly and easily, as rushing increases the stress level. Be sure to use available equipment to make the assist as easy as possible. If you are on the bottom, solve the problem there if at all possible and check your instruments to gain a more secure sense of orientation.

If you are on the surface, use positive buoyancy to make it easier to solve the problem and be sure to talk over the solution. (See figure 7-9.) Have your buddy use the easiest possible way to breathe and, if needed, help your buddy by using a simple tow through the water.

BUDDY RESCUE

The *buddy rescue* is performed when prevention, self rescue, or a buddy assist has failed or is not appropriate. They are also used when the situation would lead directly and immediately to a serious diving acci-

Fig. 7-9 Positive Buoyancy at Surface

dent, if an outsider did not intervene. These are the most difficult rescues to perform and, fortunately, the least often needed. The panicked diver or the diver who has collapsed into unconsciousness and is not breathing requires this type of rescue. However, remember that *self rescues and buddy assists make up the vast majority of all rescues*. Diver rescues involving panic or collapse are rare.

The significance of distinguishing between the buddy assist and the buddy rescue relates directly to human values. During a buddy assist, neither the victim nor the rescuer is in any great danger. The assist is easy for the rescuer and does not embarrass the victim. However, during a buddy rescue, both the victim and rescuer are in real danger, particularly the victim. Such a rescue is extremely difficult and requires considerable outside help and support. This rescue will make great demands on your personal resources of skill, strength, and courage. Everyday life does not prepare most people for dealing with such emergencies.

The assist and rescue have similar techniques. Often a rescue becomes an assist as soon as the victim calms down or, sometimes, the diver being assisted ends up needing to be rescued. Most often, you or your buddy perform assists and rescues, but in some cases, an instructor, lifeguard, boat crew, or even a passing diver will handle the situation. This may happen because an outside person is better qualified, physically or mentally, to make a rescue, because the buddies are separated, or because both buddies are in trouble.

The rescue primarily uses diving skills you have already learned. These skills do not require great precision, but they do require added urgency because your buddy may have panicked or be unconscious. Most of the *additional* skills you need in a rescue are common first aid techniques. Specifically, these skills include:

1. All buddy assist skills
2. Handling a struggling buddy underwater or on the surface
3. Bringing an unconscious buddy to the surface
4. Handling an unconscious buddy on the surface
5. Mouth-to-mouth artificial respiration in the water
6. Cardiopulmonary resuscitation (CPR)
7. Taking care of yourself during a buddy rescue
8. Searching for a missing diver

Struggling and Panic

Your buddy may quickly progress from a state of stress, to struggling, to panic. As soon as you are aware of a problem, move in, and assist your buddy. The effects, signs, or symptoms of stress will be your clues to trouble. If your buddy is already struggling or is panicked, you must take care to protect yourself. Think quickly before acting, then take action, always leaving yourself a way out, if the situation should become out of control.

The worst panic situation is underwater, because your buddy might
take your regulator mouthpiece or
knock off your mask. Fortunately,
you will probably never see a
panicked diver underwater. In many
underwater panic cases, the diver's
survival instinct overpowers proper
training and the diver tries to escape
to the surface.

If you are helping your buddy underwater and the situation does get out
of control, push away, and take care
of yourself. If this does not work or
does not seem reasonable, make
your buddy positively buoyant, if at
all possible, by ditching the weight
belt and inflating the buoyancy control device. (See figure 7-10.) Next,

Fig. 7-10
Ditching Buddy's Weight Belt

do the same for yourself so you are also positively buoyant. Now you both
can go to the surface and sort out the situation. A mechanical inflator and an
octopus regulator are extremely valuable in such a situation.

A struggling diver on the surface is still dangerous, but you have more options for the rescue. Again, stop and think before acting. If your buddy is
struggling and has not yet panicked, or you see the cause of the difficulty
and believe you can immediately help, move in and act. Your physical
contact and action may stop the panic and bring the situation under control.
Whenever possible, use positive buoyancy for your own protection.

If the situation is more desperate and you are unsure you can be effective or
safe when reaching your buddy, approach from where your buddy can see
you; stop, and shout clear, but brief instructions. Try to make your buddy
relax and take action. If your buddy swims toward you, simply back up
toward safety to the boat or shore.

If your buddy does grab you and you are in distress, first attempt to break
away by pushing off from your buddy with your hand or foot. (See figure 7-
11.) Another method is to go underwater, as this is the last place a panicked
diver wants to go. Still another method is to continue with the immediate
goal of the rescue — positive buoyancy. Ditch your buddy's weights and
inflate both buoyancy control devices. These actions can be done in any
order, but it is best, if possible, to help your buddy first. If you have a surface
float, give it to your buddy.

During panic, divers cannot help themselves, but if you wait until your buddy
collapses from struggling, then you may have to deal with a drowning. If your
talking or actions do not work and panic persists, you may want to go onto
scuba and approach your buddy from underwater and behind. In this case,

Fig. 7-11 Pushing Away

ditch your buddy's weights and inflate the buoyancy compensator with no further talk and no help from your buddy. After doing this, back off until the situation calms down.

When your buddy is no longer struggling, you can proceed with other assistance, such as towing to safety. Do not concern yourself with the fine details or skillful form during a rescue. Just get your buddy safely buoyant at the surface and ready to end the dive.

Unconscious Diver

The most serious situation you will ever face is when your buddy is unconscious. In the water, unconsciousness is usually accompanied by lack of respiration. Speed becomes critical in this situation. You must immediately bring your buddy to the surface, open the airway, and start mouth-to-mouth artificial respiration, while you prepare to leave the water as soon as possible.

It is very unlikely that your buddy will become unconscious and stop breathing while you are diving side-by-side underwater. More likely, you may find your buddy on the bottom not breathing after you have become separated.

Approach and hold your buddy as quickly as possible. If your buddy is entangled or gear is in the way, remove it. You have no way to reasonably control your unconscious buddy's exhalation during the ascent, but your buddy will die without air. So, speed to the surface is a must. Immediately establish maximum positive buoyancy for your buddy, hold him or her from

Fig. 7-12 Bringing Unconscious Diver to Surface

the rear or side, push off the bottom, and swim for the surface. (See figure 7-12.) If you feel you are working too hard, ditch your own weights and/or inflate your buoyancy control device.

If you lose control during the ascent, take care of yourself first. Let go of your buddy, slow down, relax, and be sure to exhale. Your buddy will float to the surface and, as soon as you regain control, you can proceed with the rescue.

During the ascent, it may be helpful to tilt your buddy's head back to open the airway and, if the regulator is already in the mouth, to hold it there. However, these are fine details of technique that are not of proven value. Getting to the surface immediately *is* of proven value.

Once on the surface, float your buddy on his or her back and tilt the head back to open the airway. You may have to roll your buddy over to open the airway. Spontaneous breathing often starts at this point. If it does not, and there is a pulse, start mouth-to-mouth artificial respiration. If there is no pulse, expedite to a place where you can perform CPR.

Missing Diver

Someday, your buddy or some other diver in your group may be missing. It is human nature to want to take immediate action and have every available diver enter the water for the search. This is both a dangerous and an ineffective way to find the missing diver. As with most other diving emergencies, stop, think, get control, then take action. First, get the answers to several vital questions. Who is with the missing diver? Where was the missing diver last seen? When did the dive start and when was the diver missed? How much air did the missing diver have? What kind of equipment was the missing diver using? Did the missing diver have any known difficulties? Who is available, equipped, and qualified to search for the missing diver?

If the dive is being done from a dive boat with an underwater sound recall system, this should be used before any search is begun. The search plan should use only qualified divers who have the experience, equipment, and no decompression problems. Buddy pairs start the search in the area the diver was last seen. A safety diver with a surface float should be stationed on the surface and someone on the surface should be in charge of the operation. (Note figure 7-13.) During the search, other details can be arranged, such as special equipment, communications, and transportation.

If the search is not successful in a short time, the plan should be changed and local authorities advised. How long the search lasts is determined by how much air was in the missing diver's tank.

It is possible that you may be the only other person involved and your buddy is missing. In this case, you have all the necessary information. You are limited by your own resources of experience, equipment, skill, endurance, and air supply. Do not risk your own safety in a poorly organized search, but do what you can. If you are not successful, get help and notify the proper authorities.

Fig. 7-13 Search for Missing Diver

HELICOPTER EVACUATION

Serious boating or diving accidents sometimes require that the injured person be evacuated by helicopter. This is usually done by the U.S. Coast Guard, but military or police helicopters may also do rescues. When you know medical care is needed, contact the Coast Guard as soon as possible and work out a plan. Follow their instructions. Use the radio frequency 2182 kHz, VHF channel 16, or other frequencies specified by the Coast Guard. Continuously listen to the radio after the plan has begun.

Advise the helicopter of the location before it arrives so the pilot can make a proper approach. Display a distress signal on the boat so the helicopter knows which boat has requested help.

Select and clear the most suitable hoist area, which will probably be the stern. If the boat has no clear deck area, it may be necessary to tow a dinghy or raft behind. If the hoist is at night, light the area as well as possible. Be sure you do not shine any lights on the helicopter and blind the pilot. If there are obstructions in the vicinity, put a light on them so the pilot can see them.

Next, secure all loose gear and remove any antennas or poles that might be in the way. Be sure you can still communicate on the radio after you remove the antennas. There will be a high noise level under the helicopter, so conversation between the deck crew will be almost impossible. Arrange a set of hand signals between those who will be assisting. Change course to permit the craft to ride as easily as possible with the wind 20 degrees on the port bow if possible. Reduce speed if necessary to ease the boat's motion, but maintain steerage. The best possible speed is 10 to 15 knots.

If you do not have radio contact with the helicopter, signal a "come on" when you are in all respects ready for the hoist. Use a flashlight at night. Allow the basket or stretcher to touch down on the deck prior to handling to avoid static shock. If a trail line is dropped by the helicopter, guide the basket or stretcher to the deck with the line. The line will not cause shock.

Place the person in the basket sitting with hands clear of the sides or strap the person in the stretcher. Place a lifejacket on the person if possible. Signal the helicopter hoist operator when ready for hoist. The person in the basket or stretcher should nod if able. Deck personnel then give the "thumbs up" signal.

If it is necessary to take the stretcher away from the hoist point, unhook the hoist cable and keep it free for the helicopter to haul in the hoist cable. Do not secure the cable to the vessel or attempt to move the stretcher without unhooking it. When the person is strapped in the stretcher, signal the helicopter to lower the cable, hook up again, and signal the hoist operator when ready to hoist. Keep the stretcher from swinging or turning. If a trail line is attached to the basket or stretcher, use it to steady. Keep clear of the line. Be sure to send complete information on any person who is a victim of a diving accident.

It is good to remember that a boat may be further away from help than you would be on a shore dive, but the boat provides far greater support in an emergency.

RESCUE SKILLS

You can learn many rescue skills by taking general public safety courses, such as swimming, lifesaving, first aid, and CPR. These are offered throughout the country by the Red Cross, YMCA, recreation departments, schools, and other institutions. These courses can help you improve your knowledge and ability in the water and be better prepared to help people when they are in need.

Swimming, lifesaving, and first aid courses are recommended with a word of caution. These courses are for the general public; they are not designed for divers. Many good strokes for normal swimming and lifesaving skills are not useful for divers. The diving environment, activities, and equipment give divers complications and advantages that regular lifesavers do not have. Of all these courses, first aid is the most useful and applies the most directly to diving. Advanced diving courses provide the best training for diver rescue.

TOWS

Tows include various techniques for moving a diver who needs help through the water to a safer place, either boat or shore. While towing, you become aware of environmental and other complications that make rescues difficult. Several important principles make diving rescue tows more effective. Some of these are shown in figure 7-14.

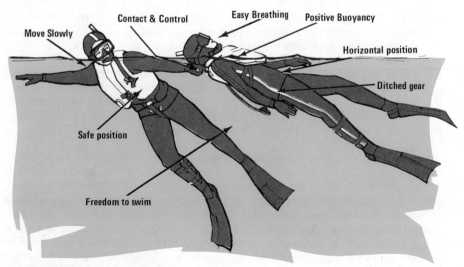

Fig. 7-14 Principles of Towing

1. Provide your buddy with the best, most appropriate way to breathe, by giving mouth-to-mouth artificial respiration, by keeping mouth and nose clear and well above the water, and by using scuba and/or snorkel, depending on conditions.
2. Keep your buddy at or near the horizontal position in the water. This allows you to move much easier than if your buddy is upright in the water.
3. Stay in contact with your buddy and control him or her during the tow.
4. Use a tow which gives you the greatest freedom and safety to swim and still effectively care for your buddy.
5. Use positive buoyancy.
6. Take your time. You still need to pace yourself, even when your buddy is not breathing.
7. Ditch any equipment which hinders the tow, such as game bag, spear, camera, tank, and so forth.
8. Have your buddy help by relaxing and doing an easy fin kick, if possible.
9. Use your own equipment for a smoother rescue, such as the compass to navigate, scuba to breathe, buoyancy control device to control buoyancy, and so forth.
10. If possible, have someone help you tow and perform mouth-to-mouth artificial respiration.
11. Change positions and fin kicks as needed to relieve muscle fatigue, provide more buddy contact, and ease the stress. Towing can be done from your buddy's side, head, or feet. Fin kicks while towing can be done on your front, side, or back; and you can change between flutter, scissors, and frog kicks.

Tows do not require the fine detail of a graceful, synchronized swimming performance. These tows are crude but effective ways to help another diver. By remembering these principles, you can do nearly anything to get the job done. Most divers find certain techniques and positions work better than others. Still, the details are left up to you — whatever works.

Towing beside your buddy, as shown in figure 7-15, is the position used most often. The most common way to do this is to place your hand in your buddy's armpit. Use the hand which is closest to your buddy. Then swim side-by-side in the normal position or on your side while your buddy is on his or her back. You can also place your arm through the armpit and hold the tank valve, pack, wet

Fig. 7-15 Side-by-Side Towing

suit, or back of the neck. However, your buddy feels better when you make physical contact rather than holding gear. This is the best position for mouth-to-mouth resuscitation and the close physical contact gives your buddy the most reassurance. You can also watch your partner's face, easily talk to each other, and see where you are going.

You can also *tow or push another diver from the feet.* These tows are usually for tired, but calm, divers. Your buddy places his or her fins on your shoulders while keeping the legs straight. You then hold the knees and simply swim while pushing. A variation is to have your diving partner hold onto your shoulders while keeping both legs straight, then lie back with the legs spread and let you swim while pushing, as shown in figure 7-16. An advantage of these tows is that you can see where you are going.

Tows from your buddy's head are done when he or she is conscious and breathing. These tows are often faster and easier to perform than the others, but they do not necessarily give the close physical contact or directional control of the other tows. You may hold onto your buddy with one hand on the buoyancy control device, tank valve, wet suit neck, a strap, hood, hair, or chin. You can hold your buddy's head with both hands. This method gives you better contact and your buddy is more reassured, but swimming and directional control are more difficult. A note of caution: when towing by the buoyancy control device or part of the wet suit, you may interfere with the other diver's breathing. Take the time to be sure your buddy is okay.

Fig. 7-16 Towing by Pushing Technique

All the tows described so far are almost always done with your buddy floating faceup; but, when you use a surface float, as shown in figure 7-17, your buddy can lie facedown and breathe with the snorkel or regulator. These are easy tows for tired divers.

When two divers are available to make a rescue, one should be at the victim's side for artificial respiration and towing and one should be positioned at the victim's head for towing. When three divers make a rescue, one is at the victim's head for towing; one is at the victim's side for artificial respiration and towing; and one stays at the victim's other side for towing, ditching gear, artificial respiration, and relief. Your compass can be used with most tows so you do not have to watch your destination; you can watch your buddy and still maintain directional control.

LEAVING THE WATER

If your buddy can still function, but is just tired, simply give a helping hand when getting out of the water at the end of the assist or rescue. If your partner is unable to help, then obtain outside help, if at all possible.

First, remove all possible equipment from your buddy. Then, remove your own equipment if your buddy still needs help leaving the water. If entering a boat, have all available people securely hold your buddy and carefully lift him or her into the boat.

Fig. 7-17 Towing with Surface Float

If you both are diving alone from a small boat, the task is more difficult. After you remove all possible equipment, place both of your buddy's hands on the boat gunwale, as shown in figure 7-18. Be sure his or her face is above the water. Now, while holding your buddy's hands in place, give a strong kick with your fins and climb into the boat. Next, grab your buddy's wrists and pull and/or drag your buddy over the gunwale to the waist, then roll your buddy the rest of the way into the boat. You have to be careful not to capsize a small boat while doing this and you may have to deflate both buoyancy control devices.

Fig. 7-18 Bringing Buddy to Boat

If your rescue goes to the shore rather than to a boat, ditch maximum equipment and obtain outside help if your partner is unable to help. If you are alone in this situation, hold your buddy from behind with both of your arms through his or her armpits and drag your buddy backward onto shore, as shown in figure 7-19.

ARTIFICIAL RESPIRATION

When your buddy is not breathing, you need to immediately start artificial respiration. Mouth-to-mouth is the best method and can be done both in and out of the water. Figure 7-20 shows the steps of mouth-to-mouth artificial respiration when done out of the water. The principles are the same in the water, but some added techniques are needed and it is always best to have someone help you. Use a surface float, if available, to increase your buoyancy and control.

Fig. 7-19 Bringing buddy to Shore

1. Start by placing the victim on his back and wiping away any visible foreign matter in his mouth.

2. Then, open the airway by tilting the victim's head back. Put one hand under the neck and lift; put the other hand on the forehead and push down. This extends the victim's neck and provides an open airway by moving the tongue away from the back of the throat.

3. To restore breathing, pinch the victim's nose with the thumb and forefinger of the hand on the victim's forehead. Pinching the nose prevents air from escaping; pressing on the forehead maintains the head-back position.

4. Next, open your mouth widely, take a deep breath, seal your mouth tightly around the victim's and, with your mouth forming a wide-open circle, blow into the victim's mouth 12 times per minute. For small children and infants, puff gently into both the nose and mouth about 20 times per minute.

5. Watch the victim's chest as it rises. After exhaling, raise your mouth, turn your head to the side, and listen for the victim to exhale. Watch his chest to see that it falls.

6. If the chest is not rising and falling, something is wrong. Check again for foreign matter stuck in the victim's mouth. Recheck the position of his head and jaw. If the stomach is bulging, turn the victim's head to the side and press down on the upper abdomen just below the rib cage.

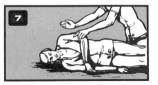

7. If air still cannot pass in and out of the victim's lungs, turn him onto his side and administer sharp blows with the heel of your hand between the shoulder blades. The blows may jar any obstructions free.

Fig. 7-20 Mouth-to-Mouth Artificial Respiration

As soon as you realize your buddy is not breathing, or you arrive at the surface after rescuing your buddy underwater, open the airway by tilting your buddy's head back with the jaw forward. If breathing does not begin, give your buddy two to six quick breaths while ditching gear and increasing buoyancy. Turn his or her head partly to one side so you do not have to get as high out of the water. Good buoyancy control devices are important in this situation. Place your nearest hand through your buddy's armpit and hold the tank valve, pack, buoyancy control device, or back of your buddy's neck, as shown in figure 7-21. Your nearest hand is your right hand if you are on your buddy's right side and the left hand for the left side. Your free hand rests on your buddy's forehead to help maintain the head position and close the nose while you inflate the lungs.

Seal your buddy's nose with your fingers, cover the mouth with your mouth, and exhale forcefully approximately 12 times per minute. If you push too hard

Fig. 7-21 Mouth-to-Mouth Artificial Respiration in Water

Fig. 7-22 Mouth-to-Snorkel Artificial Respiration

and your buddy's head goes underwater, there is no danger as long as you have sealed or covered both nose and mouth. Watch your buddy's chest to be sure it rises each time you blow. This indicates an exchange of air. After each of your exhalations, remove your mouth so your buddy can exhale.

Your buddy may vomit during artificial respiration. If this happens, stop, turn his or her head to the side, clear the mouth with your fingers, and continue. If for some reason you cannot blow through the mouth, hold your hand over it and blow through the nose.

Continue mouth-to-mouth artificial respiration until breathing resumes or you are relieved. You can tow and do this technique at the same time, but it is difficult — you need help. Because your buddy will need to be treated for shock, will need medical care, and may need CPR, get out of the water as soon as possible.

If conditions of extreme surface chop, inadequate buoyancy control devices, a long distance to swim, or a combination of these prevail, a snorkel-to-mouth resuscitation may be needed. In this case, you swim near your buddy's head and hold the snorkel mouthpiece in your buddy's mouth. Both of you are on your backs. You swim while blowing alternately down the open end of the snorkel tube. (See figure 7-22.)

CARDIOPULMONARY RESUSCITATION

If the victim's *heart stops beating, blood circulation needs to be restored*. Cardiopulmonary resuscitation is a combination of mouth-to-mouth artificial respiration and external cardiac compression. It is the most extensive first aid treatment you will probably be called upon to perform.

If your buddy is not breathing, and you do not detect any pulse, or you are unable to perform mouth-to-mouth artificial respiration in the water, you should tow your buddy as fast as possible to the nearest place where you can get out of the water and administer CPR. It cannot be done in the water.

The technique includes opening the airway and doing mouth-to-mouth artificial respiration, with the addition of closed chest/heart compression. Cardiac compression consists of compressing or pushing on the heart, as shown in figure 7-23. When you press on the lower breastbone, you squeeze the heart between the breastbone and the backbone. This forces blood out of the heart and into the arteries. When you stop pressing, blood automatically refills the heart through incoming veins. Constant repetition (approximately 60 times per minute) of this squeeze-release process keeps the heart beating artificially.

When combined with mouth-to-mouth artificial respiration, one or two rescuers can perform both heart (cardio) and lung (pulmonary) resuscitation, as shown in figure 7-24.

It is extremely difficult, if not impossible, to check for the victim's pulse in the water. The carotid (neck) pulse is the most useful, but a slow or weak pulse

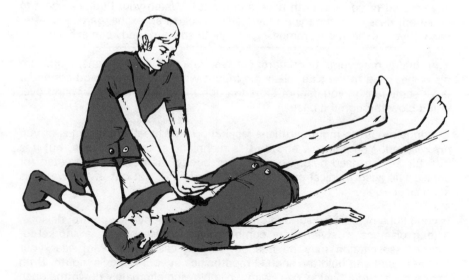

Fig. 7-23 External Cardiac Compression

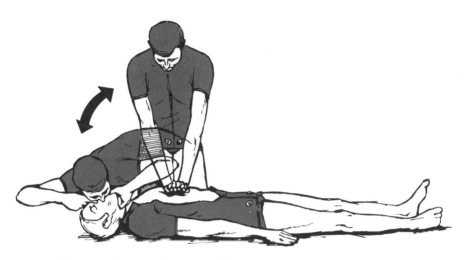

Fig. 7-24 Cardiopulmonary Resuscitation

may not be detected, particularly in cold water. Dilation of the pupils may also provide a secondary check for lack of circulation, but this should not be relied upon as an absolute indicator.

The information given here is only an overview of CPR. *The technique can only be learned after several hours of training with a qualified instructor.* Exact performance of CPR is critical because severe damage to internal organs can result when pressure is improperly applied to the chest. All divers are advised to attend a CPR course. These courses provide more details and extensive practice with mannequins. Never practice heart compression on an actual person. Schedules of course offerings are available by calling the local American Heart Association or Red Cross.

FIRST AID

First aid is best defined as "the immediate and temporary care of an injured person." First aid is *not* medical care. First aid is needed between the time of rescue and professional medical care.

Standard first aid training is very valuable for divers, as nearly all standard first aid procedures apply to diving. There are a few additions for diving maladies. You owe it to yourself and those around you to take a first aid course, to have good first aid books on hand, and to have a diving first aid kit. (See figure 7-25.)

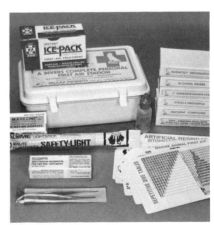

Fig. 7-25 Diving First Aid Kit

Behind all first aid efforts is the all-important aspect of caring about people. In diving, you care enough to help your diving buddy, with whom you already have a special relationship. To be most effective at first aid, you need to make direct physical and mental contact. Deal first with the important problems, such as breathing, bleeding, embolism, and shock, and let medical personnel handle the details.

As with all diving emergencies, stop and think. Do what you can, taking care to not cause further injury; but do not attempt to replace a doctor. For example, you do not need to diagnose which kind of emphysema your buddy has. If you know what happened and can see the obvious symptoms of a lung overpressure incident, proceed with first aid for air embolism.

The most serious accidents peculiar to diving are caused by pressure changes such as, decompression sickness, air embolism, and related injuries. The first aid for these is the same.

1. Have victim lay down on a slope with feet slightly higher than the head and with the body tilted toward the left side.
2. Continuously administer pure oxyen.
3. Provide first aid for shock.
4. Give artificial respiration, if needed.
5. Get medical assistance, if possible.
6. Transport to a chamber as soon as possible.

Wounds

Probably the most common injuries in diving are simple wounds: scrapes, cuts, bruises, and so forth. Wounds may be caused by rocks, equipment, or aquatic life. These are most often caused by diver carelessness and usually are not nearly as serious as embolism, shock, and decompression sickness. Most wounds are handled by getting out of the water, washing the area with soap and warm water, applying antiseptic, bandaging, and using followup medical care, if needed. Consideraton should be given to possible infection with any wound.

If a diver is bleeding excessively, control it by pressing directly on the wound, elevating the body part, applying pressure to points in the groin and armpits, or applying a tourniquet and leaving it in place. (See figure 7-26.) Any serious bleeding requires first aid for shock and medical attention.

Shock

Shock is a depressed condition of the body's functions when a person is injured. Shock can add to or aggravate another injury and, in fact, can be serious by itself. The greater the injury, the greater the possibilities of shock. In diving accidents requiring rescue, simply presume there is shock and treat for it. All first aid for shock is compatible with the first aid for any special diving injuries.

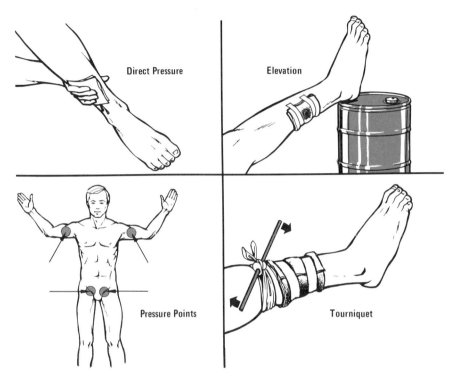

Fig. 7-26 Control of Bleeding

1. Have victim lie down with feet slightly higher than the head.
2. Make close physical and mental contact with the victim, and be reassuring, while keeping the victim as comfortable as possible.
3. Keep the victim warm, but not hot.
4. Give fluids if the victim is conscious and can take them.
5. Give first aid for any other injuries, bleeding, embolism, and so forth.
6. Be ready to give mouth-to-mouth artificial respiration at any time.
7. Do not leave the victim alone.
8. Get medical help.
9. Transport to medical care.

Other Possible Problems Needing First Aid

Other possible incidents requiring first aid include problems with heat and cold, infections, seasickness, and fractures. These can vary from annoyances to serious accidents. Only those of most concern to divers are covered here.

Fractures, strains, or sprains rarely occur in the water with diving activities, but they may occur while climbing a cliff near the dive site. Immobilize the injury and joints on both sides of the injury by splinting. Treat for shock and get medical attention. Again, standard first aid training is the best preparation for this problem.

Excessive heat can cause heat stroke or heat exhaustion. These are greater problems in the tropics, but they can also happen on a hot day when you are wearing a wet suit out of the water in the sun. Stroke is a serious condition characterized by a high temperature, hot, flushed skin, and possible collapse. Treat strokes by cooling the entire body as rapidly as possible. This includes removing clothing, drinking fluids, bathing the body with cool water, and resting in a cool, shady area. Get medical attention as soon as possible.

Heat exhaustion is not as serious and the symptoms differ from heat stroke. The victim feels uncomfortable, hot, fatigued, dizzy, nauseated, faint, and has cool clammy skin. Treat for shock by letting the victim rest in a cool, shady area while giving fluids and salt.

Sunburn can ruin any vacation. Sand and water glare increase the likelihood of sunburn for divers. You need to beware of surface snorkeling without protection on your back and legs. Wearing clothing and wet suits in the water will help prevent sunburn. Also, apply sunscreen frequently, particularly if you have been in and out of the water. For minor sunburn, a cool damp cloth or cold shower will give some relief; but for more severe sunburns, it is necessary to exclude air with a dry, sterile dressing and to seek medical attention.

Seasickness can be caused by motion in, on, or under the water. The victim feels nauseated, weak, and generally ill. You can help prevent seasickness in yourself by taking motion sickness pills before entering or traveling on the water, eating light and easily digestible meals, getting plenty of fresh air while on the water, or sleeping during boat trips.

External ear infections are often caused by not drying or cleaning the ears after repeated diving, particularly in warm or tropical diving areas. The outer ear becomes red, painful, and tender. Medical care and not diving for some time cures an ear infection. This infection can be prevented by keeping the ears dry and clean. In certain problem diving areas, such as the tropics, a dilute alcohol rinse may be used, or a special commercial preparation can also decrease external ear infections.

Mere knowledge of rescue techniques is not enough to insure that you will be able to help a diver in a real-life situation. Training and repeated practice can increase both your physical and mental ability to make rescues. It is best to practice in open water rather than pools, so you will be more familiar and comfortable with the environmental conditions. Hopefully, you will never encounter a circumstance requiring diver rescue, but with the combination of proper knowledge, training, and skill, you will be prepared to do anything from simply assisting your buddy to saving a life.

PART VIII
deep diving

introduction

As you become more experienced as a diver, you continually expand your horizons and range of experiences. One of the most probable areas of your increased diving activity may be in the deeper water. Deep diving has a fascination of its own beyond the usual diving activities done at normal depths.

Most beginning diver training is conducted in less than 40 feet of water. Sixty feet can be considered the limit of shallow diving, a good limit for most diver training and a reasonable limit for the novice diver. One hundred feet is a reasonable limit for divers with some experience. It is generally understood that shallow diving ranges from 0 to 60 feet, with deep sport diving being the range from 60 to 100 feet. Actually, the range of 60 to 100 feet could better be defined as *deeper water diving* and dives made beyond 100 feet considered *true* deep dives.

Sport diving is not recommended beyond 100 feet. But sport divers do dive between 100 and 190 feet. Dives beyond 100 feet are ordinarily better left to paid professional divers. Diving from 100 to 190 feet requires extreme caution, with particular attention to air supplies, decompression, narcosis, and surface support. For sport divers, diving beyond 190 feet is not considered at all reasonable.

Some reasons for *not* diving deep include increased air consumption and breathing resistance, need for decompression, and risk of nitrogen narcosis. With all the sensible reasons for *not* diving deep, why do experienced divers still regularly make deep dives? The reasons often include the same feelings generally experienced by all divers, but in deep diving, these feelings are intensified. These include the challenge, adventure, escape, opportunity to explore, an interest in the environment, and other sensations possibly heightened by nitrogen narcosis. Other reasons are more objective, often because the goal of the dive happens to be in deeper water.

deep diving conditions, preparation, the deep dive, decompression

Definitions of deep diving and recommendations on diving limits vary with water conditions and geographic location, however, increasing pressure affects the *physiology* of the body in the same manner no matter where you dive.

As a diver, you have a responsibility to yourself, your buddy, other divers, and the diving community. In order to meet this responsibility, you should understand your depth limitations and deep diving conditions. You should also prepare properly for deep diving, make the deep dive with proper care, and have an understanding of decompression procedures. (See figure 8-1.) The material presented here is intended to help prepare you for deep diving so you will meet this responsibility.

Fig. 8-1 Divers Decompressing

Depth (Feet)	Pressure (Atmospheres) (Absolute)	Reduction of Air Supply	No Decompression Limits (Minutes)	Decompression Stops Needed On Single Tank	Safe Emergency Ascent Possibilities	U.S. Navy Recommended Air Demand Open Circuit Scuba Use	Divers First Physically Notice Nitrogen Narcosis
30 (33)	2	1/2	None	Not Needed	Very Easy	--	None
60 (66)	3	1/3	60	Unlikely	Easy	Normal Working Limit	Some Divers
100 (99)	4	1/4	25	Possible	Difficult	--	Many Divers
130 (132)	5	. 1/5	10	Very Possible	Very Difficult	Maximum Working Limit	Most Divers

Fig. 8-2 Variables at Different Depths

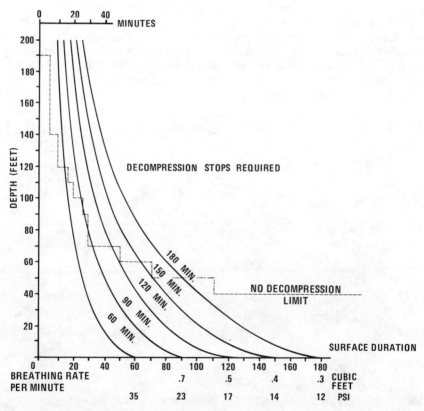

Fig. 8-3 Air Consumption at Depth

Figure 8-2 details some of the variables to be considered as you dive deeper. As pressure in atmospheres and no-decompression limits do not correspond exactly, both depths are provided.

DEEP DIVING CONDITIONS

AIR CONSUMPTION AND BREATHING RESISTANCE

Pressure increases with depth and more air is required to equalize the pressure. This reduces the duration of the air supply, as shown in figure 8-3. As dives become truly deep in the 100- to 190-foot range, additional air supplies at the surface and double tanks should be considered.

Many factors influence the rate of air consumption, making it difficult to compute. These factors include the diver's physical size, experience, fitness, breathing habits, and stress level. Swimming or work load, water temperature and depth, breathing resistance, and air losses due to leaks, equalizing, and buoyancy control also affect air consumption.

The important consideration is not precisely the air consumption at any given *moment*, but what *cutoff point* should be used to have more than enough air for ascending, decompression, and any surface difficulties.

Breathing resistance, like air consumption, also increases with depth. (See figure 8-4.) Greater depth and pressure mean that denser air must be moved through the regulator and the diver's body. It is possible for divers to demand more air than the regulator can apparently supply under certain conditions. These conditions include greater depths (over 100 feet), low tank pressures (less than 500 psi), high respiration rates (breathing rapidly), and poor regulator maintenance. Accident reports reveal many so-called "out-of-air" situations actually occur when divers misuse their regulators under these conditions.

120 FEET

Fig. 8-4 Breathing Resistance

ENVIRONMENT

Deeper dives often allow you to avoid surface conditions such as chop, surf, or surge, in addition to currents. Caution needs to be exercised with currents because the bottom and surface currents may run in different directions and at different speeds. Also, if you cover a great deal of horizontal distance and surface far from the starting point, you may have a difficult surface swim back to your exit point.

Wet suits provide less warmth and buoyancy at depth because the increased pressure compresses them. The loss of protection combined with colder water temperatures causes you to lose heat, so you therefore lose more energy. You may need to use a thicker wet suit and add a hood, boots, and gloves when making a deep dive. The loss of buoyancy at depth requires that you use a buoyancy control device.

Sunlight is filtered out so there is less available light and less apparent color at depth. The clarity of the water is often better at depth as the water is less affected by surface conditions. The visibility can be severely limited when the loss of light and turbid water are combined at depth. These environmental conditions are shown in figure 8-5.

Fig. 8-5 Environmental Conditions

Even though there is usually less aquatic life, there are some fish, shells, corals, and other animals that live only at greater depths.

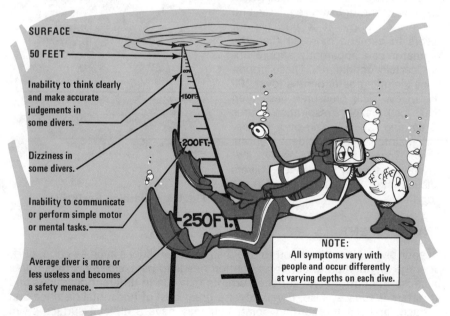

Fig. 8-6 Nitrogen Narcosis Symptoms

DECOMPRESSION SICKNESS

Decompression sickness is a significant problem of deeper water diving. It will be dealt with in great detail later in this section.

NITROGEN NARCOSIS

Nitrogen narcosis is a lethargy, or euphoria, brought on by breathing the nitrogen of compressed air in the presence of carbon dioxide while under pressure. It also has been called "rapture of the deep." The exact mechanism causing nitrogen narcosis is not known.

The physical effects of narcosis are usually first observed between 100 and 130 feet, but they gradually increase with increasing depth and first affect the ability to reason. Other symptoms of nitrogen narcosis include loss of judgment and skill, false sense of well being, lack of concern for safety, difficulty in accomplishing tasks, foolish behavior or inappropriate actions, loss of memory and, in severe cases, semi-consciousness. (Note figure 8-6.)

The same diver may have different effects from day to day and they may vary extensively from diver to diver. Narcosis will also vary greatly depending on the environmental conditions. Extensive diving experience and good physical condition tend to decrease the effects of nitrogen narcosis, while the use of drugs and fatigue have definite adverse effects. Nitrogen narcosis has been compared to the use of alcohol and may appear to be similar to alcoholic intoxication.

Nitrogen narcosis has no aftereffects, although it has been noted that the symptoms do not wear off immediately with some people. Also, the loss of memory may make it difficult to accurately remember the dive. The real danger lies in what might go wrong while the diver is under the effects of nitrogen narcosis at depth.

You should treat nitrogen narcosis by ascending to shallower water and prevent nitrogen narcosis by avoiding deep diving where it may affect you. When you do dive deep, be prepared to deal with nitrogen narcosis by diving with a buddy, being physically fit, trained, experienced, having a dive plan and proper equipment, and, above all, taking it slow and easy.

OTHER HAZARDS

There are several hazards well-known to divers who stay above 100 feet. Deep diving exaggerates the effects of some of these. You need to be more concerned with these when you make deep dives. These hazards include:

1. Carbon dioxide excess
2. Carbon monoxide poisoning
3. Use of prescription, non-prescription, and illegal drugs
4. Use of alcohol before diving
5. Cold and fatigue
6. Increased diver stress

In addition to being hazards in themselves, each of these hazards can contribute to decompression sickness and nitrogen narcosis.

DEEP DIVING PREPARATION

Careful preparation will greatly improve the safety and enjoyment of the deep dive. Fitness, training, experience, planning, communications, and equipment all need to be superior to common practice for shallow dives.

PERSONAL FITNESS

Because deep diving imposes new stresses and physiological changes on you, it is important to be in top physical condition. This includes having maintained good fitness through adequate rest, well-balanced diet, and regular exercise.

It is particularly important in deep diving to avoid harmful habits, including the use of any type of drugs, smoking, and drinking. No alcohol should be consumed for at least 12 hours prior to the dive. If you regularly take some medication and know the side effects, its continued use should not be a particular problem provided you are careful and aware of the effects. If you have any doubts, consult your doctor.

Immediately prior to diving, you should have a good night's sleep and eat a good meal both the night before and the morning of the dive. It is also wise to repeatedly equalize the pressure in your ears in the 24-hour period before diving. This will make equalization much easier during the dive itself. *If you are not feeling well, you should not dive at all.* You should have a good attitude about making the particular deep dive.

TRAINING AND EXPERIENCE

After your first scuba diving course, you should seek out other diving courses to gain additional understanding and experience under instructor supervision. These courses will carry names such as "open water diver," "advanced diver," "specialty diver," and others. (See figure 8-7.)

It is extremely important to gradually build your experience prior to deep diving. This includes slowly increasing your range of skills, activities, and depth. If you stop diving for awhile, you need to decrease your diving depth and then gradually increase depth again. How often you

Fig. 8-7 Additional Training

dive also affects how susceptible you will be to both nitrogen narcosis and decompression sickness.

DIVE PLANNING

The dive plan is a tool you should use for safer and more enjoyable diving. A dive plan can be very simple and ver- bally handled between two buddies for most dives. But, when making dives with a greater degree of risk, such as deep diving, the dive plan will need to be more detailed with some parts of it being written. (See figure 8-8.)

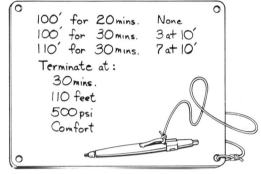

100' for 20mins. None
100' for 30mins. 3 at 10'
110' for 30mins. 7 at 10'
Terminate at:
30mins.
110 feet
500 psi
Comfort

Fig. 8-8 Decompression and Termination Information

Your first step is to find a buddy and decide on a time and place for the dive, along with a dive objective. You and your buddy should work out details of who, what, when, where, why, and how. Some aspects of the dive plan need particular attention for a deep dive:

1. Notify someone who is not going with you of your dive plans.

2. Select a simple objective for the dive.

3. Locate the nearest operational chamber and know the quickest way to reach it in an emergency.

4. Carefully check weather and sea conditions.

5. Work out and record a decompression plan with an alternate plan in case you go over your time or depth.

6. Establish strict criteria for terminating the dive: tank pressure (minimum), depth (maximum), time (maximum), and comfort.

7. Reserve the right to make the decision not to dive at any time, based on changing personal, medical, or environmental conditions.

COMMUNICATIONS

Communication methods are limited for sport divers by either the cost or the ineffectiveness of most electronic and mechanical devices. You and your buddy should definitely carry a slate and pencil. These need to be carefully secured so they will not be lost during the dive. Pertinent information, particularly decompression and alternate plans, should be recorded on the back of the slate before the dive. The other side of the slate can be used for underwater communication.

Fig. 8-9 Standard Hand Signal

The standard diver hand signals should be reviewed to make sure you both are using the same signals. (See figure 8-9.) Additional hand signals may be added as agreed upon for the particular dive.

EQUIPMENT

Proper selection, use, and care of equipment is extremely important in deep diving. Changes to existing equipment and additional equipment will be required.

The scuba regulator should be single hose, top of the manufacturer's line, with a submersible pressure gauge. It should also have an extra second stage (octopus) or some other alternate breathing system, such as a pony bottle. You should carefully care for your regulator and take it in to be professionally overhauled at least once a year. The octopus regulator is important for any out-of-air situation, but particularly when decompression is needed. No deep dive should ever be made without a submersible pressure gauge. It is the primary safety tool for planning and executing the deep dive.

Standard tanks, ranging in size from 70 to 80 cubic feet, are the most commonly used for sport diving, including deep diving. You should consider double tank units when you make dives to extreme depths. You may also want to consider J-valves as a back-up in case you forget to check the submersible pressure gauge.

Fig. 8-10 Equipment for Deep Dive

Equipment, as shown in figure 8-10, which gives information, becomes much more important on the deep dive. In addition to the submersible pressure gauge, you and your buddy should have a depth gauge, watch, and compass. For added safety and efficiency, many divers use a bottom timer that automatically records the time of the dive. Serious deep divers use two depth gauges for each diver: a capillary gauge for accurate reading in shallow water during decompression, and a dial-reading depth gauge for easier reading at greater depths.

The decompression meter also can be a valuable tool when intelligently used. It is a delicate instrument that attempts to duplicate the complex changes going on in your body during the dive. It is most useful for multilevel dives of less than 100 feet and with less than six hours of surface intervals. The meter should be calibrated yearly, checked against the U.S. Navy Diving Tables, properly handled, protected from decreased pressure (as in an airplane), kept out of the sun, compared with other meters, and used with the depth gauge, watch, and tables. It can become difficult to arrange and observe so many gauges and instruments. Therefore, you can conveniently place your instruments on a console which attaches to the end of the submersible pressure gauge hose. (See figure 8-11.)

Fig. 8-11 Instrument Panel

Fig. 8-12 Buddy Gear Check

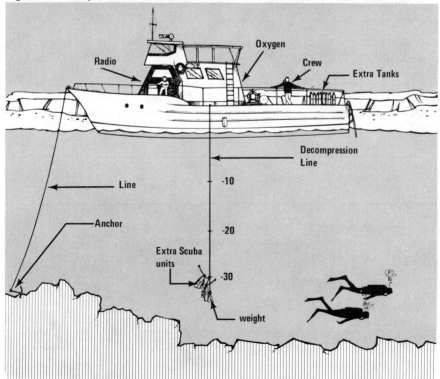

Fig. 8-13 Surface Support for Deep Diving

Other diving accessories should be kept to a minimum, consistent with the objective of the dive, so as not to get in the way and detract from a safe dive. The knife is a safety tool and should be used on all dives. Also, due to the decreased light intensity, an underwater light, even in daytime, is often useful on a deep dive. You and your buddy should both carefully check over your own and the other's gear prior to any dive, as shown in figure 8-12. This buddy gear check should be done with particular care prior to a deep dive.

Surface Support Equipment

Under ideal conditions for deep diving, a surface support boat would be anchored above the dive site. This, of course is not always possible, so much deep diving is done from shore. For *extremely* deep dives (100 feet or more), you should use a boat. It should be anchored directly above the dive site, as shown in figure 8-13, with the anchor line used for ascending and descending. A decompression line separate from the anchor line, weighted, marked with dye or knots at 10-foot intervals, with an extra scuba unit for each diver and extra weights, should also be hung over the side near the center of the boat. This will make decompression much safer and easier.

On board the boat, the crew can handle equipment and supply safety divers, additional air supplies, and oxygen for emergencies. A complete set of plastic decompression tables with instructions and a radio for use if a decompression chamber is needed should also be in the boat.

THE DEEP DIVE

After having set some reasonable depth limits based on your understanding of deep diving conditions and having made the necessary preparations for the deep dive, you are now ready to dive.

DESCENDING

At the surface, you do a final buddy check, making sure both you and your buddy are completely ready for the dive. You should equalize pressure in your ears at this time, even though you have not yet started your descent. When you are both ready, you should go onto scuba and record the time on your slate. Next, completely deflate your buoyancy control device and exhale to start your descent.

If at all possible, descend all the way feet-first, as shown in figure 8-14. If this is not possible, due to buoyancy, do a head-first surface dive and, as soon as the wet suit has been slightly compressed and you are negatively buoyant, continue on down feet-first. The feet-first position makes it easier to equalize pressure in your ears, provides better orientation, and provides more efficient breathing.

If you are following the anchor line down, use it to assist in your descent and to provide orientation. If you are diving from shore, you can follow the bottom contour out into deep water. If sinking straight to depth in open water, proceed feet-first, taking it slow and easy, while using your bubbles and your buddy to help provide orientation. On all descents, use the buoyancy control device to control buoyancy so you are not too negatively buoyant and continually clear your ears.

The Navy prescribes a maximum of 75 feet per minute for descending. This allows divers to clear their ears and not become disoriented by rapid pressure changes. Be sure to maintain visual or physical contact with your buddy and use the anchor line, the bottom, or your bubbles to aid in orientation. As you descend, check your depth gauge to make sure you are not exceeding the depth of the planned dive.

Fig. 8-14 Descent for Deep Dive

AT DEPTH

When you arrive at the bottom, relax. Kneel or sit down and breathe easily while adjusting to the depth and becoming oriented. Check yourself, your gear, your instruments, your buddy, and the environment. (See figure 8-15.)

Communicate and make sure you are both comfortable and conditions are within the dive plan. Because of the depth, sensations will change and you may notice a taste to the air or a distinct difference in the sound of the exhaust bubbles. Let these sensations sink in and then focus on the objective of your dive.

The wet suit loses some buoyancy at depth, which makes you heavier. To help offset this, you can remove some weight from your belt before deep diving, but do not remove so much that you lose shallow depth neutral buoyancy if you need to make decompression stops.

Fig. 8-15 Checking Conditions at Depth

Inflate your buoyancy control device for neutral buoyancy and be sure to maintain neutral buoyancy throughout the deep dive. Use a mechanical inflator which enables you to use tank air to inflate your buoyancy control device. This makes buoyancy adjustments quicker and easier to control.

Maintain your contact and orientation with your buddy, with the line you use to descend, with the bottom, or by the use of your compass. Your pace should be slow and easy, just as your breathing should be slow, deep, and relaxed. Do not attempt any hard work at depth. If you feel yourself over-breathing, stop, breathe easy, think, and get control.

NOTE: *It is particularly important to not make any dive plan changes that would increase depth or time while under the influence of nitrogen narcosis at depth.*

Continue checking conditions, controlling buoyancy, and maintaining contact and orientation. Proceed with your dive objective, being prepared at all times to terminate the dive if any problem should develop or if you reach the limits of your plan. When you are ready to make a direct ascent to the surface, be sure you are neutrally buoyant and in contact with your buddy. Breathe easy, make a final check of instruments, record the time, and proceed to ascend.

ASCENDING

The ascent may be done on the an-chor line, by following the bottom slope, or in open water, by using a combination of buoyancy control and swimming. It also is helpful to start the ascent by pushing off the bottom in open water.

The ascent rate of 60 feet per minute is far slower than most divers realize. The inflator on your buoyancy con-trol device should be in your hand so you can vent off expanding air as you ascend. (See figure 8-16.) By staying below your smallest bubbles and monitoring your gauges, you should be able to maintain the required ascent rate. Maintain contact with your buddy and keep your orientation by using the bottom, the anchor line, or your bubbles. The entire ascent should be very slow and easy.

Fig. 8-16 Ascent Procedure

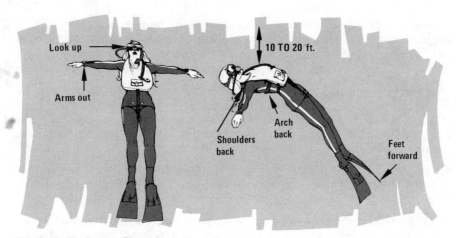

Fig. 8-17 Flaring to Slow Ascent

When approaching the surface, dump the air in your buoyancy control device and flare, if necessary, to slow your ascent. (See figure 8-17.) If the dive requires decompression, or if you are going to decompress for safety sake, use one of the methods outlined in the following section on decompression. The essence of the entire deep dive is one of slow, easy diving while maintaining buddy contact and orientation.

DECOMPRESSION

The need for decompression has been well understood for many years. Nitrogen is taken up by the body during every scuba dive. The amount absorbed depends on the depth and duration of the dive. If the quantity of nitrogen dissolved in the tissues and blood exceeds a certain critical amount, the diver must ascend slowly or make stops along the way to allow the tissues to remove the excess nitrogen. If this is not done, nitrogen bubbles will remain in the blood and tissues after the dive, causing decompression sickness (also called the "bends," "caisson disease," "chokes," or "compressed air illness").

More recent research indicates that *all* decreases in pressure cause bubble formation from the inert nitrogen coming out of solution. This and the increased understanding of the number of variables that increase the likelihood of decompression sickness have necessitated that sport divers take a more careful and conservative approach to decompression.

DECOMPRESSION SICKNESS

Decompression sickness is due to inadequate decompression. This may be caused by improper use of the tables, inaccurate determination of time or depth, exceeding the standard tables, exceeding the 60-foot per minute ascent rate, missing or not accurately timing decompression stops, or improper use of a decompression meter. In addition to these causes, there are factors which may increase the likelihood of decompression sickness. These include: age (usually over 40), obesity, fatigue, alcohol or drug use before or immediately after the dive, old injuries which cause poor circulation, poor physical condition, illness, heavy work during or immediately after the dive, water temperature extremes (particularly a cold dive or a hot shower immediately after the dive), smoking immediately after the dive, dehydration, pregnancy, and restricting blood flow by having an arm or leg in a cramped position.

Symptoms

Decompression sickness symptoms usually start within a short period following the dive. As shown in figure 8-18, 50 percent of symptoms usually occur within 30 minutes, 85 percent usually occur within 1 hour, 95 percent usually occur within 3 hours, 1 percent may be delayed more than 6 hours, and if over 24 hours have passed since the dive, it is probably not decompression sickness.

The symptoms vary due to the location of bubble formation and can occur while still under pressure. The most common symptom is local pain in the arms or legs. The more serious symptoms which involve the central nervous system include pain, unconsciousness, shock, vertigo, visual difficulty, nausea/vomiting, hearing difficulty, speech difficulty, lack of balance, numbness, weakness, strange sensations, and shortness of breath.

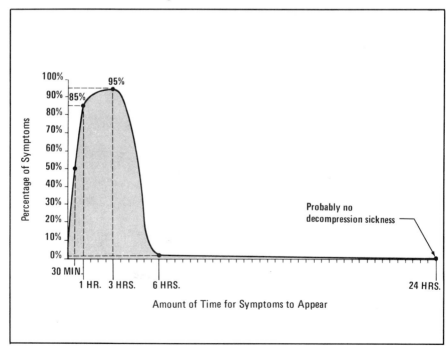

Fig. 8-18 Rates of Decompression Sickness

Treatment

Decompression sickness is a serious diving malady, fortunately, it responds very well to proper treatment. Most cases are not fatal, but serious and irreversible damage can be done if immediate and adequate treatment is not provided. If decompression sickness is suspected due to the symptoms and/or the nature of the dive, proceed immediately with the following:

1. Have the victim lie down with feet slightly higher than the head, and with the body tilted onto the left side.
2. Continuously administer pure oxygen. This helps wash the nitrogen from the system.
3. Provide first aid treatment for shock, including keeping the victim warm.
4. Give artificial respiration if required.
5. Get emergency medical assistance.
6. Call ahead to the decompression chamber.
7. Transport as soon as possible to the chamber. (See figure 8-19.) If this will be by air, the helicopter or other aircraft should be flown as low as possible.
8. It is not safe to attempt treatment of decompression sickness in the water.

Fig. 8-19 Recompression Chamber

Prevention

Decompression sickness can be prevented by avoiding deep dives or dives which require decompression stops, particularly if those are repetitive dives. All deep dives should be carefully planned and divers should understand and use the U.S. Navy Decompression Tables. However, bear in mind that the U.S. Navy Decompression Tables have no built-in safety factor. They have been designed and tested on a special and narrowly defined group of people — male Navy divers, 20 to 30 years old. In addition, these divers are in good physical condition, highly motivated, and trained. Sport divers, on the other hand, include a complete cross-section of the general public: teenagers, older people, women, minority groups, and others, most of whom are not in as good physical condition as Navy divers. (See figure 8-20.)

Fig. 8-20 Different Physical Characteristics

Whenever in doubt, or if some factor increases the likelihood of decompression sickness, you should err on the safe side by increasing decompression by using the next greater time and depth in the tables.

Maintaining good personal fitness and using complete proper equipment will also help. All scuba dives should have a rate of ascent not exceeding 60 feet per minute. By ascending at this rate, you are actually decompressing. In addition, prevention should include avoiding all possible factors which might increase the chance of decompression sickness.

DECOMPRESSION TABLES

To make the U.S. Navy Decompression Tables easier to understand, some key definitions need to be kept in mind. (The tables are shown in figures 8-21 through 8-23.) *Decompression* is a release from pressure and *decompression tables* are devised to allow for a controlled release from pressure to avoid the symptoms of decompression sickness. To *recompress* is to put back under pressure. This is done during the treatment of decompression sickness. *Chambers* are referred to as decompression, recompression, or hyperbaric chambers.

NO-DECOMPRESSION LIMITS AND REPETITIVE GROUP DESIGNATION TABLE FOR NO-DECOMPRESSION AIR DIVES

Depth (feet)	No-decompression limits (min)	A	B	C	D	E	F	G	H	I	J	K	L	M	N	O
10		60	120	210	300											
15		35	70	110	160	225	350									
20		25	50	75	100	135	180	240	325							
25		20	35	55	75	100	125	160	195	245	315					
30	NA	15	30	45	60	75	95	120	145	170	205	250	310			
35	310	5	15	25	40	50	60	80	100	120	140	160	190	220	270	310
40	200	5	15	25	30	40	50	70	80	100	110	130	150	170	200	
50	100		10	15	25	30	40	50	60	70	80	90	100			
60	60		10	15	20	25	30	40	50	55	60					
70	50			5	10	15	20	30	35	40	45	50				
80	40			5	10	15	20	25	30	35	40					
90	30			5	10	12	15	20	25	30						
100	25			5	7	10	15	20	22	25						
110	20				5	10	13	15	20							
120	15				5	10	12	15								
130	10				5	8	10									
140	10				5	7	10									
150	5				5											
160	5					5										
170	5					5										
180	5					5										
190	5					5										

Fig. 8-21 No-Decompression Limits Table

RESIDUAL NITROGEN TIMETABLE FOR REPETITIVE AIR DIVES

*Dives following surface intervals of more than 12 hours are
not repetitive dives. Use actual bottom times in the Standard
Air Decompression Tables to compute decompression for
such dives.

															A	0:10
																12:00*
														B	0:10	2:11
														2:10	12:00*
												C	0:10	1:40	2:50
												1:39	2:49	12:00*
										D	0:10	1:10	2:39	5:49
									1:09	2:38	5:48	12:00*
							E	0:10	0:55	1:58	3:23	6:33
							0:54	1:57	3:22	6:32	12:00*
					F	0:10	0:46	1:30	2:29	3:58	7:06
					0:40	1:15	1:59	2:58	4:25	7:35	12:00*
			G	0:10	0:41	1:16	2:00	2:59	4:26	7:36
			0:36	1:06	1:41	2:23	3:20	4:49	7:59	12:00*
		H	0:10	0:37	1:07	1:42	2:24	3:21	4:50	8:00
		0:33	0:59	1:29	2:02	2:44	3:43	5:12	8:21	12:00*
	I	0:10	0:34	1:00	1:30	2:03	2:45	3:44	5:13	8:22
	0:31	0:54	1:19	1:47	2:20	3:04	4:02	5:40	8:40	12:00*
J	0:10	0:32	0:55	1:20	1:48	2:21	3:05	4:03	5:41	8:41
K	0:10	0:29	0:50	1:12	1:36	2:04	2:39	3:22	4:20	5:49	8:59
	0:28	0:49	1:11	1:35	2:03	2:38	3:21	4:19	5:48	8:58	12:00*
L	0:10	0:27	0:46	1:05	1:26	1:50	2:20	2:54	3:37	4:36	6:03	9:13
	0:20	0:45	1:04	1:25	1:49	2:19	2:53	3:36	4:35	6:02	9:12	12:00*
M	0:10	0:26	0:43	1:00	1:19	1:40	2:06	2:35	3:09	3:53	4:50	6:19	9:29
	0:25	0:42	0:59	1:18	1:39	2:05	2:34	3:08	3:52	4:49	6:18	9:28	12:00*
N	0:10	0:25	0:40	0:55	1:12	1:31	1:54	2:19	2:48	3:23	4:05	5:04	6:33	9:44
	0:24	0:39	0:54	1:11	1:30	1:53	2:18	2:47	3:22	4:04	5:03	6:32	9:43	12:00*
O	0:10	0:24	0:37	0:52	1:08	1:25	1:44	2:05	2:30	3:00	3:34	4:18	5:17	6:45	9:55
	0:23	0:36	0:51	1:07	1:24	1:43	2:04	2:29	2:59	3:33	4:17	5:16	6:44	9:54	12:00*
0:10	0:23	0:35	0:49	1:03	1:19	1:37	1:56	2:18	2:43	3:11	3:46	4:30	5:28	6:57	10:06
0:22	0:34	0:48	1:02	1:18	1:36	1:55	2:17	2:42	3:10	3:45	4:29	5:27	6:56	10:05	12:00*

Repetitive group at the beginning of the surface interval

NEW → GROUP DESIGNATION

| Z | O | N | M | L | K | J | I | H | G | F | E | D | C | B | A |

REPETITIVE DIVE DEPTH

40	257	241	213	187	161	138	116	101	87	73	61	49	37	25	17	7
50	169	160	142	124	111	99	87	76	66	56	47	38	29	21	13	6
60	122	117	107	97	88	79	70	61	52	44	36	30	24	17	11	5
70	100	96	87	80	72	64	57	50	43	37	31	26	20	15	9	4
80	84	80	73	68	61	54	48	43	38	32	28	23	18	13	8	4
90	73	70	64	58	53	47	43	38	33	29	24	20	16	11	7	3
100	64	62	57	52	48	43	38	34	30	26	22	18	14	10	7	3
110	57	55	51	47	42	38	34	31	27	24	20	16	13	10	6	3
120	52	50	46	43	39	35	32	28	25	21	18	15	12	9	6	3
130	46	44	40	38	35	31	28	25	22	19	16	13	11	8	6	3
140	42	40	38	35	32	29	26	23	20	18	15	12	10	7	5	2
150	40	38	35	32	30	27	24	22	19	17	14	12	9	7	5	2
160	37	36	33	31	28	26	23	20	18	16	13	11	9	6	4	2
170	35	34	31	29	26	24	22	19	17	15	13	10	8	6	4	2
180	32	31	29	27	25	22	20	18	16	14	12	10	8	6	4	2
190	31	30	28	26	24	21	19	17	15	13	11	10	8	6	4	2

RESIDUAL NITROGEN TIMES (MINUTES)

Fig. 8-22 Residual Nitrogen Timetable

U.S. NAVY STANDARD AIR DECOMPRESSION TABLE

Depth (feet)	Bottom time (min)	Time first stop (min:sec)	Decompression stops (feet)					Total ascent (min:sec)	Repetitive group
			50	40	30	20	10		
40	200						0	0:40	*
	210	0:30					2	2:40	N
	230	0:30					7	7:40	N
	250	0:30					11	11:40	O
	270	0:30					15	15:40	O
	300	0:30					19	19:40	Z
	360	0:30					23	23:40	**
	480	0:30					41	41:40	**
	720	0:30					69	69:40	**
50	100						0	0:50	*
	110	0:40					3	3:50	L
	120	0:40					5	5:50	M
	140	0:40					10	10:50	M
	160	0:40					21	21:50	N
	180	0:40					29	29:50	O
	200	0:40					35	35:50	O
	220	0:40					40	40:50	Z
	240	0:40					47	47:50	Z
60	60						0	1:00	*
	70	0:50					2	3:00	K
	80	0:50					7	8:00	L
	100	0:50					14	15:00	M
	120	0:50					26	27:00	N
	140	0:50					39	40:00	O
	160	0:50					48	49:00	Z
	180	0:50					56	57:00	Z
	200	0:40				1	69	71:00	Z
	240	0:40				2	79	82:00	**
	360	0:40				20	119	140:00	**
	480	0:40				44	148	193:00	**
	720	0:40				78	187	266:00	**
70	50						0	1:10	*
	60	1:00					8	9:10	K
	70	1:00					14	15:10	L
	80	1:00					18	19:10	M
	90	1:00					23	24:10	N
	100	1:00					33	34:10	N
	110	0:50				2	41	44:10	O
	120	0:50				4	47	52:10	O
	130	0:50				6	52	59:10	O
	140	0:50				8	56	65:10	Z
	150	0:50				9	61	71:10	Z
	160	0:50				13	72	86:10	Z
	170	0:50				19	79	99:10	Z
80	40						0	1:20	*
	50	1:10					10	11:20	K
	60	1:10					17	18:20	L
	70	1:10					23	24:20	M
	80	1:00				2	31	34:20	N
	90	1:00				7	39	47:20	N
	100	1:00				11	46	58:20	O
	110	1:00				13	53	67:20	O
	120	1:00				17	56	74:20	Z
	130	1:00				19	63	83:20	Z
	140	1:00				26	69	96:20	Z
	150	1:00				32	77	110:20	Z
	180	1:00				35	85	121:20	**
	240	0:50			6	52	120	179:20	**
	360	0:50			29	90	160	280:20	**
	480	0:50			59	107	187	354:20	**
	720	0:40		17	108	142	187	455:20	**

Fig. 8-23 Standard Air Decompression Table

* See No Decompression Table for repetitive groups
** Repetitive dives may not follow exceptional exposure dives

U.S. NAVY STANDARD AIR DECOMPRESSION TABLE

Depth (feet)	Bottom time (min)	Time to first stop (min:sec)	70	60	50	40	30	20	10	Total ascent (min:sec)	Repetitive group
90	30								0	1:30	*
	40	1:20							7	8:30	J
	50	1:20							18	19:30	L
	60	1:20							25	26:30	M
	70	1:10						7	30	38:30	N
	80	1:10						13	40	54:30	N
	90	1:10						18	48	67:30	O
	100	1:10						21	54	76:30	Z
	110	1:10						24	61	86:30	Z
	120	1:10						32	68	101:30	Z
	130	1:00					5	36	74	116:30	Z
100	25								0	1:40	*
	30	1:30							3	4:40	I
	40	1:30							15	16:40	K
	50	1:20						2	24	27:40	L
	60	1:20						9	28	38:40	N
	70	1:20						17	39	57:40	O
	80	1:20						23	48	72:40	O
	90	1:10					3	23	57	84:40	Z
	100	1:10					7	23	66	97:40	Z
	110	1:10					10	34	72	117:40	Z
	120	1:10					12	41	78	132:40	Z
	180	1:00				1	29	53	118	202:40	**
	240	1:00				14	42	84	142	283:40	**
	360	0:50			2	42	73	111	187	416:40	**
	480	0:50			21	61	91	142	187	503:40	**
	720	0:50			55	106	122	142	187	613:40	**
110	20								0	1:50	*
	25	1:40							3	4:50	H
	30	1:40							7	8:50	J
	40	1:30						2	21	24:50	L
	50	1:30						8	26	35:50	M
	60	1:30						18	36	55:50	N
	70	1:20					1	23	48	73:50	O
	80	1:20					7	23	57	88:50	Z
	90	1:20					12	30	64	107:50	Z
	100	1:20					15	37	72	125:50	Z
120	15								0	2:00	*
	20	1:50							2	4:00	H
	25	1:50							6	8:00	I
	30	1:50							14	16:00	J
	40	1:40						5	25	32:00	L
	50	1:40						15	31	48:00	N
	60	1:30					2	22	45	71:00	O
	70	1:30					9	23	55	89:00	O
	80	1:30					15	27	63	107:00	Z
	90	1:30					19	37	74	132:00	Z
	100	1:30					23	45	80	150:00	Z
	120	1:20				10	19	47	98	176:00	**
	180	1:10			5	27	37	76	137	284:00	**
	240	1:10			23	35	60	97	179	396:00	**
	360	1:00		18	45	64	93	142	187	551:00	**
	480	0:50	3	41	64	93	122	142	187	654:00	**
	720	0:50	32	74	100	114	122	142	187	773:00	**
130	10								0	2:10	*
	15	2:00							1	3:10	F
	20	2:00							4	6:10	H
	25	2:00							10	12:10	J
	30	1:50						3	18	23:10	M
	40	1:50						10	25	37:10	N
	50	1:40					3	21	37	63:10	O
	60	1:40					9	23	52	86:10	Z
	70	1:40					16	24	61	103:10	Z
	80	1:30				3	19	35	72	131:10	Z
	90	1:30				8	19	45	80	154:10	Z

Decompression stops (feet)

*See No Decompression Table for repetitive groups
**Repetitive dives may not follow exceptional exposure dives

When using the decompression tables, *bottom time*, as shown in figure 8-24, is the time from leaving the surface until the diver starts a *direct ascent* back to the surface. *Depth* is figured as the deepest point reached during the dive. A *repetitive dive* is a second, or subsequent, dive made in less than 12 hours. Dives made more than 12 hours apart are counted as single dives. The time between repetitive dives is called the *surface interval*. Surface intervals are shown in the Residual Nitrogen Timetable, figure 8-22. As nitrogen is lost both during decompression and the surface interval, this time is taken into account when using the tables.

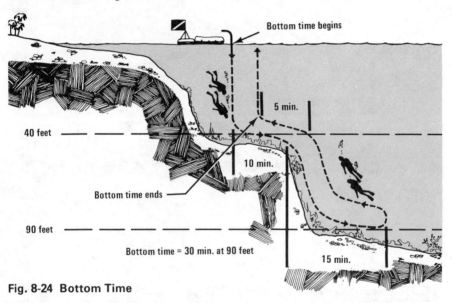

Fig. 8-24 Bottom Time

Residual nitrogen is that nitrogen left in your body after the dive. It could be compared to alcohol in the body which is gradually absorbed and consumed by the body until it is gone. In a similar manner, this residual nitrogen is gradually given off by your body until a normal nitrogen level is reached. To keep track of this residual nitrogen, after you have completed the first dive and a surface interval, the residual nitrogen is expressed as an amount of time you have already apparently spent at each possible depth before the next dive. This is provided in a table.

The decompression tables list *repetitive group letters*. These letters are arbitrary symbols established to help you compute how much nitrogen is still in your body. They start with "A" and go through "O," and then skip to "Z." "A" represents the least amount of nitrogen and "Z" the most. Therefore, each letter of the alphabet represents a certain amount of residual or leftover nitrogen you need to account for on repetitive dives.

The term *decompression schedule* is used by the Navy when referring to a particular depth and time in the decompression tables, such as, 130 feet for

15 minutes would be a 130/15 decompression schedule. (See figure 8-23.) A *decompression stop* is also called "stage decompression." These stops are set out in 10-foot increments in the decompression tables and are used to allow gradual nitrogen release. A *"no-decompression dive"* is one that does not require these decompression stops.

Using the Tables

With the definitions in mind, some procedures should be reviewed. The maximum rate of ascent from compressed air scuba dives is 60 feet per minute; that is, one foot per second, which is a very slow rate. It can be gauged by staying behind the smallest bubbles and using your watch and depth gauge in combination.

When using the decompression tables, *always round off both time and depth to the next greater time or depth.* The tables have no safety factor and rounding off to a smaller number or interpolating may be cutting you short and putting you in a potentially unsafe situation.

The "no-decompression" limits, as shown in figure 8-25, should be used by sport divers to avoid decompression. Even though a dive is a "no-decompression dive," there still is residual nitrogen in the diver's system. When diving to less than 33 feet, all dives are "no-decompression dives." The deepest a diver can possibly go without having to make decompression stops is 190 feet for 5 minutes. It will take a sport diver almost five minutes to reach 190 feet, let alone actually doing anything at that depth.

NO-DECOMPRESSION LIMITS AND REPETITIVE GROUP DESIGNATION TABLE FOR NO-DECOMPRESSION AIR DIVES

Depth (feet)	No-decompression limits (min)	A	B	C	D	E	F	G	H	I	J	K	L	M	N	O
10		60	120	210	300											
15		35	70	110	160	225	350									
20		25	50	75	100	135	180	240	325							
25		20	35	55	75	100	125	160	195	245	315					
30	NA	15	30	45	60	75	95	120	145	170	205	250	310			
35	310	5	15	25	40	50	60	80	100	120	140	160	190	220	270	310
40	200	5	15	25	30	40	50	70	80	100	110	130	150	170	200	
50	100		10	15	25	30	40	50	60	70	80	90	100			
60	60		10	15	20	25	30	40	50	55	60					
70	50		5	10	15	20	30	35	40	45	50					
80	40		5	10	15	20	25	30	35	40						
90	30		5	10	12	15	20	25	30							
100	25		5	7	10	15	20	22	25							
110	20			5	10	13	15	20								
120	15			5	10	12	15									
130	10			5	8	10										
140	10			5	7	10										
150	5			5												
160	5				5											
170	5				5											
180	5				5											
190	5				5											

Fig. 8-25 No-Decompression Limits

All *depths* in the U.S. Navy Decompression Tables are in feet. All *times* in the decompression tables are in minutes with the exception of the surface interval table, which uses hours and minutes. Decompression stops are at 10-foot intervals. The deepest stop is at 50 feet and the shallowest is at 10 feet. When you are decompressing, the chest should be kept at the depth of the decompression stop.

The minimum surface interval used in the U.S. Navy Tables is 10 minutes. If dives are made less than 10 minutes apart, then the time of the two dives is added together and the greatest depth of the two dives is used to compute decompression.

An exception to the U.S. Navy Decompression Tables occurs when a repetitive dive is made to the *same or greater depth* than the previous dive, and the *surface interval is short* enough that the residual nitrogen time is greater than the actual bottom time of the previous dive. In this case, add the actual bottom time of the previous dive to the actual bottom time of the repetitive dive and decompress for the total bottom time and the deepest depth. For example, a dive was made to 70 feet for 50 minutes, with a surface interval of 30 minutes, and a repeat dive to 70 feet for 40 minutes is planned. The first dive left the diver in the "J" group. Following the repetitive dive table for a "J" group diver with a 30-minute surface interval to return to 70 feet, we find the residual nitrogen time is 57 minutes. Therefore, instead of adding the 57 minutes from the table, we use the actual bottom time for the first dive (50 minutes) and add it to the planned bottom time (40 minutes), for a total bottom time of 90 minutes at 70 feet. This puts the diver into a decompression situation requiring a decompression stop of 23 minutes at 10 feet. However, if the 57 minutes from the table were used, the diver would have to decompress for 33 minutes at 10 feet.

This exception occurs as it is not possible to build into the U.S. Navy Decompression Tables every conceivable combination of dives. If you disregard this exception and handle the tables in the normal manner, rather than by the procedure listed here, your error will be on the safe side, as you will be decreasing your diving time if you are making no-decompression dives, or increasing the amount of time you spend decompressing.

Avoiding Decompression Stops

There are several ways you can effectively use the decompression tables and deal with the problem of decompression. Making the first dive the *deeper* dive will aid in decompression as each successive shallower dive will actually be helping you decompress. Also, the procedure of going to maximum depth first during any one dive, spending a limited time there, and then moving to shallow water, will aid in decompression.

Diving to less than 33 feet does not require decompression stops. Repeated dives can be made in this depth range without significant concern about decompression, or, if deeper dives have been made earlier in the day, then you can safely make subsequent dives in this lesser depth range. Making the surface intervals between dives as long as possible will also aid in eliminating nitrogen and increasing diving safety.

Sport divers should not devise their own system for modifying the U.S. Navy Decompression Tables. The Navy has a proven system for what they call "cold or arduous" dives. This system can be used to modify the tables for any factor that might increase the likelihood of decompression sickness. The procedure is to use the *next greater depth and time* rather than that actually indicated by the dive. This may cause you to decompress when you otherwise would not have done so or it may decrease your dive time. It provides that needed margin of safety. In addition, many divers pause at 10 feet before surfacing as an added safety precaution, even when decompression stops are not required.

A procedure that does not modify the tables, but does provide a margin of safety during no-decompression dives is to reduce your in-water time by moving one repetitive letter back from the maximum allowed in the no-decompression table. (See figure 8-26.)

NO-DECOMPRESSION LIMITS AND REPETITIVE GROUP DESIGNATION TABLE FOR NO-DECOMPRESSION AIR DIVES

Depth (feet)	No-decompression limits (min)	A	B	C	D	E	F	G	H	I	J	K	L	M	N	O
10		60	120	210	300											
15		35	70	110	160	225	350									
20		25	50	75	100	135	180	240	325							
25		20	35	55	75	100	125	160	195	245	315					
30	NA	15	30	45	60	75	95	120	145	170	205	250	310			
35	310	5	15	25	40	50	60	80	100	120	140	160	190	220	270	310
40	200	5	15	25	30	40	50	70	80	100	110	130	150	170	200	
50	100			10	15	25	30	40	50	60	70	80	90	100		
60	60			10	15	20	25	30	40	50	55	60				
70	50			5	10	15	20	30	35	40	45	50				
80	40			5	10	15	20	25	30	35	40					
90	30			5	10	12	15	20	25	30						
100	25			5	7	10	15	20	22	25						
110	20				5	10	13	15	20							
120	15				5	10	12	15								
130	10				5	8	10									
140	10				5	7	10									
150	5				5											
160	5					5										
170	5					5										
180	5					5										
190	5					5										

Note: Move back one repetitive group letter from maximum indicated and use that as your maximum.

Fig. 8-26 Repetitive No-Decompression Diving Safety Procedure

You can avoid decompression stops by using the decompression meter as a "no-decompression" meter. Keep the meter's needle or indicator out of the red (decompression range). Even though the meter does *not* indicate the need for decompression, but you are concerned that some condition may increase the likelihood of decompression sickness, you can pause at 10 feet and allow the meter to pass the distance between two arbitrary points you establish. These points might be the distance between a mark and a letter, as shown in figure 8-27.

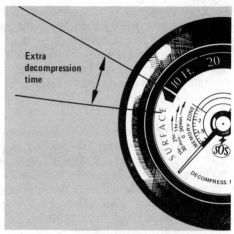

Fig. 8-27 Use of Decompression Meter

High Altitude Diving

There are some special situations concerning deep and decompression diving which you should understand. The decompression tables were made for diving in salt water at sea level. Therefore, they are *not* designed for fresh water lakes at high altitudes. As fresh water is slightly less dense than salt water, there will be a slight error on the safe side when using the decompression tables in fresh water, *if* that fresh water is at, or near, sea level.

Several altitude tables having modifications to the U.S. Navy Decompression Tables have appeared in diving periodicals or technical publications. These tables are not tested, but are simply mathematical computations. You should carefully review these tables before diving in lakes at high altitudes and use large safety margins.

Flying after Diving

The best recommendation for flying after diving is to wait at least 12 hours before you fly, although the U.S. National Oceanic and Atmospheric Administration states that a scuba diver should wait at sea level for a surface interval long enough to be classified as a Group "D" diver. If you make all "no-decompression" dives during the day, you can fly in a commercial jet after a four-hour surface interval. It is far better though, to wait as long as possible before flying after diving, because if you are at the margin of being safe in a cabin pressurized to 8,000 feet while flying at 30,000 feet and the cabin loses its pressurization, you may get the bends. Caution should also be used when flying in General Aviation airplanes. Many of these airplanes are now pressurized and would present the same problem if they suddenly lost pressurization.

Bounce Dives

A "bounce dive" usually refers to a deep dive made very quickly. Such a dive might be made to check an anchor or pick up a piece of equipment. The bounce dive must be counted just as any other scuba dive as far as decompression requirements are concerned. Sport divers also do a great deal of "multilevel" diving, as shown in figure 8-24. They may reach a maximum depth of 95 feet on the dive, but spend most of their time at 60 feet and actually be at 40 feet during part of the dive. The U.S. Navy Decompression Tables do not allow for this mode of diving as the entire dive is counted at the greatest depth.

DECOMPRESSION PROCEDURES

The ideal method for actually decompressing from a deep dive, is to use a decompression line hung from a boat or to use the boat's anchor line. The

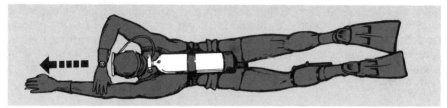

Fig. 8-28 Compass Course Decompression

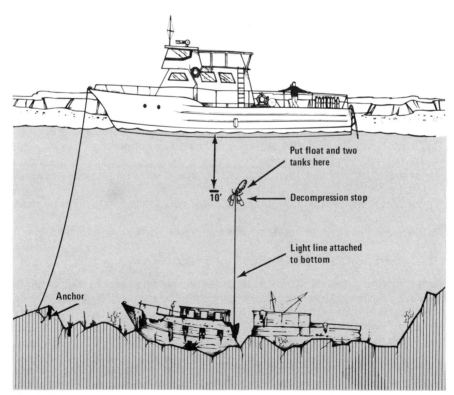

Put float and two
tanks here

10'   Decompression stop

Light line attached
to bottom

Anchor

Fig. 8-29 Decompression from the Bottom

boat could be rolling or pitching while you hold onto the line. If this is the case, you should descend on the line so your chest comes no shallower than the prescribed depth for the decompression stop. Another procedure for decompressing is to swim into shallow water and explore the bottom at the decompression depth. In open water, you may swim an underwater compass course at the decompression depth toward your exit point. (Note figure 8-28.) Still another procedure, as shown in figure 8-29, is to attach a light line at the bottom and ascend to the decompression depth while holding the line and using positive buoyancy to stay in place. This method is less affected by surface conditions.

When, for some reason, you must interrupt or omit decompression and you have no signs of decompression sickness and no recompression chamber is available, you should come to the surface, get another tank of air as quickly as possible, and return to the water. At 40 feet, remain one-fourth of the 10-foot stop listed in the decompression table. At 30 feet, remain one-third of the 10-foot stop, at 20 feet, remain one-half of the 10-foot stop, and at 10 feet, remain 1-1/2 times the scheduled 10-foot stop.

DIVE PLANNING WITH THE DECOMPRESSION TABLES

The tremendous importance of dive planning, particularly on a deep dive, has already been described. A crucial part of dive planning during the deep dive is to deal with decompression. The decompression tables can be used in a variety of ways to plan a dive and avoid or take the required decompression.

These dive planning methods include using the decompression tables in several ways.

1. To avoid decompression stops
2. To stay within a particular decompression schedule or repetitive group
3. To attain maximum depth or time on a limited air supply
4. To make minimum decompression stops
5. To make a particular dive and take whatever decompression stops are required
6. Calculate the maximum time available on a second dive without decompression
7. Calculate the minimum surface interval to avoid decompression stops

DECOMPRESSION WORKSHEETS AND DIAGRAMS

Many different types of worksheets to record decompression requirements have been devised. Most are far too complex to be useful in diving. A simple worksheet is shown in figure 8-30. This information can be listed either across the top or down the side of a 3 x 5-inch card. After the day's diving, retain the card in the logbook for future reference.

Diagramming the dive is a useful tool to visualize the day's repetitive dives. These diagrams are most often used during training to make it clear how the procedures are handled. Two such diagrams are shown in figure 8-31.

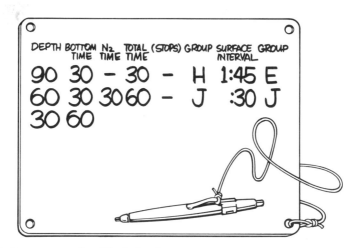

Fig. 8-30 Decompression Worksheet

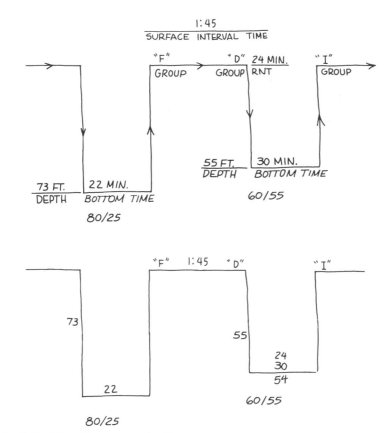

Fig. 8-31 Dive Diagram or Profile

appendix

STANDARDS FOR AIR 5.2.1.2   Air used in SCUBA operations must meet these standards of purity for the U.S. Navy. This is true no matter what the source of the air or the method used for charging the cylinders. These standards are—

Oxygen concentration	20 - 22% by volume
Carbon dioxide	0.05% (500 ppm)
Carbon monoxide	0.002% (20 ppm)
Oil—mist or vapor	5 mg per cu meter max.
Solid and liquid particles	Not detectable except as noted above under oil—mist or vapor
Odor	Not objectionable

ARCHIMEDES PRINCIPLE, GAS LAWS, AND AIR CONSUMPTION FORMULA/TABLE

Archimedes Principle: Any object wholly or partially immersed in a liquid is buoyed up by a force equal to the weight of the liquid displaced. (a) A negatively buoyant body sinks in a fluid because the weight of the fluid it displaces is less than the weight of the body. (b) A neutrally buoyant submerged body remains in equilibrium, neither rising nor sinking, because the weight of the fluid it displaces is exactly equal to its own weight. (c) A positively buoyant submerged body weighs less than the volume of liquid it displaces. It will rise and float with part of its volume above the surface. A floating body displaces its own weight of a liquid.

Boyle's Law: If the temperature is kept constant, the volume of a gas will vary inversely as the ABSOLUTE pressure while the density will vary directly as the pressure. Since the pressure and volume of a gas are inversely related—the higher the pressure, the smaller the volume, and vice-versa. The formula for Boyle's Law is:

$PV = C$

Where P= absolute pressure
V= volume
C= a constant

Charles' Law: If the pressure is kept constant, the volume of a gas will vary directly as the ABSOLUTE temperature. The amount of change in either volume or pressure is directly related to the change in absolute pressure. For example, if absolute temperature is doubled, then either the volume or the pressure is also doubled. The formula for Charles' Law is:

$PV = RT$ or $PV = R \over T$

Where P= absolute pressure
V= volume
T= absolute temperature
R= a universal constant for all gases

General Gas Law: Boyle's Law illustrates pressure/volume relationships, and Charles' Law basically describes the effect of temperature changes on pressure and/or volume. The General Gas Law is a combination of these two laws. It is used to predict the behavior of a given quantity of gas when changes may be expected in any or all of the variables. The formula for the General Gas Law is:

$$\frac{P_1 V_1}{T_1} = \frac{P_2 V_2}{T_2}$$

Where P_1 = initial pressure (absolute)
V_1 = initial volume
T_1 = initial temperature (absolute)
P_2 = final pressure (absolute)
V_2 = final volume
T_2 = final temperature (absolute)

Dalton's Law: The total pressure exerted by a mixture of gases is equal to the sum of the pressures of each of the different gases making up the mixture—each gas acting as if it alone was present and occupied the total volume. The whole is equal to the sum of its parts and each part is not affected by any of the other parts. The pressure of any gas in the mixture is proportional to the number of molecules of that gas in the total volume. The pressure of each gas is called its partial pressure (pp), meaning its part of the whole. Dalton's Law is sometimes referred to as "the law of partial pressures." The formula for Dalton's Law is:

$$P_{Total} = PP_A + PP_B + PP_C.....$$
$$and$$
$$PP_A = P_{Total} \times \frac{\%Vol._A}{100\%}$$

Where P_{Total} = Total absolute pressure of gas mixture
PP_A = Partial pressure of gas A
PP_B = Partial pressure of gas B
PP_C = Partial pressure of gas C

Henry's Law: The amount of a gas that will dissolve in a liquid at a given temperature is almost directly proportional to the partial pressure of that gas. If one unit of gas dissolves in a liquid at one atmosphere, then two units will dissolve at two atmospheres, three units at three atmospheres, etc.

AIR CONSUMPTION FORMULA

Knowing your air consumption rate is very important. By determining your consumption rate at the surface, it becomes a simple matter to calculate what it will be at any given depth. Since pressure gauges are calibrated in pounds per square inch (PSI), your consumption rate must be in PSI too. The formula is as follows:

$$\frac{PSI \div TIME}{33/33 + DEPTH/33}$$

PSI = PSI consumed in timed swim at a constant depth.

TIME = Duration of timed swim.

DEPTH = Depth of timed swim.

EXAMPLE:

A diver swims at a depth of 10 feet for 10 minutes and consumes 300 PSI of air. You want to determine his surface consumption expressed in PSI.

$$\frac{300 \ (PSI \ used) \div 10 \ (Time) = 30}{33/33 \ + 10 \ (Depth)/33 \ = 43/33} = \frac{30 \times 33}{43} = \frac{990}{43} = 23.02$$

23.02 PSI = PSI CONSUMED PER MINUTE AT SURFACE

NOTE: Consumption rate must be recalculated if tank size is changed.

AIR CONSUMPTION TABLE AT DEPTH

DEPTH IN FEET

Surface	10	15	20	25	30	40	50	60	70	80	90	100	120	140	160
15	19.5	21.8	24.0	27.0	28.5	33.0	37.5	42.0	46.5	51	55.5	60	69	78	87
16	20.8	23.2	25.6	28.8	30.4	35.2	40.0	44.8	49.6	54.4	59.2	64	73.6	83.2	92.8
17	22.1	24.7	27.2	30.6	32.3	37.4	42.5	47.6	52.7	57.8	62.9	68	78.2	88.4	98.6
18	23.4	26.1	28.8	32.4	34.2	39.6	45.0	50.4	55.8	61.2	66.6	72	82.8	93.6	104.4
19	24.7	27.6	30.4	34.2	36.1	41.8	47.5	53.2	58.9	64.6	70.3	76	87.4	98.8	110.2
20	26.	29.0	32.0	36.0	38.0	44.0	50.0	56.0	62.0	68.0	74.0	80	92	104	116
21	27.3	30.5	33.6	37.8	39.9	46.2	52.5	58.8	65.1	71.4	77.7	84	96.6	109.2	121.8
22	28.6	31.9	35.2	39.6	41.8	48.4	55.0	61.6	68.2	74.8	81.4	88	101.2	114.4	127.6
23	29.9	33.4	36.8	41.4	43.7	50.6	57.5	64.4	71.3	78.2	85.1	92	105.8	119.6	133.4
24	31.2	34.8	38.4	43.2	45.6	52.8	60.	67.2	74.4	81.6	88.8	96	110.4	124.8	139.2
25	32.5	36.3	40.0	45.0	47.5	55.0	62.5	70.0	77.5	85.0	92.5	100	115	130	145
26	33.8	37.7	41.6	46.8	49.4	57.2	65.0	72.8	80.6	88.4	96.2	104	119.6	135.2	150.8
27	35.1	39.2	43.2	48.6	51.3	59.4	67.5	75.6	83.7	91.8	99.9	108	124.2	140.4	156.6
28	36.4	40.6	44.8	50.4	53.2	61.6	70.	78.4	86.8	95.2	103.6	112	128.8	145.6	162.4
29	37.7	42.1	46.4	52.2	55.1	63.8	72.5	81.2	89.9	98.6	107.3	116	133.4	150.8	168.2
30	39.	43.5	48.0	54.	57.0	66.0	75.0	84.0	93.0	102.0	111.0	120	138	156	174
31	40.3	45.0	49.6	55.8	58.9	68.2	77.5	86.8	96.1	105.4	114.7	124	142.6	161.2	179.8
32	41.6	46.4	51.2	57.6	60.8	70.4	80.0	89.6	99.2	108.8	118.4	128	147.2	166.4	185.6
33	42.9	47.9	52.8	59.4	62.7	72.6	82.5	92.4	102.3	112.2	122.1	132	151.8	171.6	191.4
34	44.2	49.3	54.4	61.2	64.6	74.8	85.0	95.2	105.4	115.6	125.8	136	156.4	176.8	197.2
35	45.5	50.8	56.0	63.0	66.5	77.0	87.5	98.0	108.5	119.0	129.5	140	161	182	203
36	46.8	52.2	57.6	64.8	68.4	79.2	90.0	100.8	111.6	122.4	133.2	144	165.6	187.2	208.8
37	48.1	53.7	59.2	66.6	70.3	81.4	92.5	103.6	114.7	125.8	136.9	148	170.2	192.4	214.6
38	49.4	55.1	60.8	68.4	72.2	83.6	95.0	106.4	117.8	129.2	140.6	152	174.8	197.6	220.4
39	50.7	56.6	62.4	70.2	74.1	85.8	97.5	109.2	120.9	132.6	144.3	156	179.4	202.8	226.2
40	52	58.	64.0	72.0	76.0	88.0	100.	112.0	124.0	136.	148.0	160	184	208	232

CONSUMPTION RATE AT SURFACE (PSI PER MINUTE)

NO CALCULATION DIVE TABLES

TABLE 1-11 (1-6) NO DECOMPRESSION LIMITS AND REPETITIVE GROUP DESIGNATION TABLE FOR NO DECOMPRESSION AIR DIVES

Depth (feet)	10	15	20	25	30	35	40	50	60	70	80	90	100	110	120	130	140	150	160	170	180	190
No Decompression Limits (min)						310	200	100	60	50	40	30	25	20	15	10	10	5	5	5	5	5
A	60	35	25	20	15	5																
B	120	70	50	35	30	15	15	10	10	5	5	5	5									
C	210	110	75	55	45	25	25	15	15	10	10	10	7	5	5	5	5	5	5	5	5	5
D	300	160	100	75	60	40	30	25	20	15	15	12	10	10	10	8	7	5	5	5	5	5
E		225	135	100	75	50	40	30	25	20	20	15	15	13	12	10	10					
F		350	180	125	95	60	50	40	30	30	25	20	20	15	15							
G			240	160	120	80	70	50	40	35	30	25	22	20								
H			325	195	145	100	80	60	50	40	35	30	25									
I				245	170	120	100	70	55	45	40											
J				315	205	140	110	80	60	50												
K					250	160	130	90														
L					310	190	150	100														
M						220	170															
N						270	200															
O						310																

(Left margin label: REPETITIVE GROUPS)

TABLE 1-12 (1-7) SURFACE INTERVAL CREDIT TABLE

Surface interval ranges (h:min) for each repetitive group at the start of the surface interval, and the resulting new repetitive group:

Start group	Surface interval → new group
A	0:10–12:00 → A
B	0:10–2:10 → B; 2:11–12:00 → A
C	0:10–1:39 → C; 1:40–2:49 → B; 2:50–12:00 → A
D	0:10–1:09 → D; 1:10–2:38 → C; 2:39–5:48 → B; 5:49–12:00 → A
E	0:10–0:54 → E; 0:55–1:57 → D; 1:58–3:22 → C; 3:23–6:32 → B; 6:33–12:00 → A
F	0:10–0:45 → F; 0:46–1:29 → E; 1:30–2:28 → D; 2:29–3:57 → C; 3:58–7:05 → B; 7:06–12:00 → A
G	0:10–0:40 → G; 0:41–1:15 → F; 1:16–1:59 → E; 2:00–2:58 → D; 2:59–4:25 → C; 4:26–7:35 → B; 7:36–12:00 → A
H	0:10–0:36 → H; 0:37–1:06 → G; 1:07–1:41 → F; 1:42–2:23 → E; 2:24–3:20 → D; 3:21–4:49 → C; 4:50–7:59 → B; 8:00–12:00 → A
I	0:10–0:36 → I; 0:37–1:06 → H; 1:07–1:41 → G; 1:42–2:23 → F; 2:24–3:20 → E; 3:21–4:49 → D; 4:50–6:02 → C; 6:03–8:21 → B; 8:22–12:00 → A
J	0:10–0:31 → J; 0:32–0:54 → I; 0:55–1:19 → H; 1:20–1:47 → G; 1:48–2:20 → F; 2:21–3:04 → E; 3:05–4:02 → D; 4:03–5:40 → C; 5:41–8:40 → B; 8:41–12:00 → A
K	0:10–0:28 → K; 0:29–0:49 → J; 0:50–1:11 → I; 1:12–1:35 → H; 1:36–2:03 → G; 2:04–2:38 → F; 2:39–3:21 → E; 3:22–4:19 → D; 4:20–5:48 → C; 5:49–8:58 → B; 8:59–12:00 → A
L	0:10–0:26 → L; 0:27–0:45 → K; 0:46–1:04 → J; 1:05–1:25 → I; 1:26–1:49 → H; 1:50–2:19 → G; 2:20–2:53 → F; 2:54–3:36 → E; 3:37–4:35 → D; 4:36–6:02 → C; 6:03–9:12 → B; 9:13–12:00 → A
M	0:10–0:24 → M; 0:25–0:42 → L; 0:43–0:59 → K; 1:00–1:18 → J; 1:19–1:39 → I; 1:40–2:05 → H; 2:06–2:34 → G; 2:35–3:08 → F; 3:09–3:52 → E; 3:53–4:49 → D; 4:50–6:18 → C; 6:19–9:28 → B; 9:29–12:00 → A
N	0:10–0:23 → N; 0:24–0:39 → M; 0:40–0:54 → L; 0:55–1:11 → K; 1:12–1:30 → J; 1:31–1:53 → I; 1:54–2:18 → H; 2:19–2:47 → G; 2:48–3:22 → F; 3:23–4:04 → E; 4:05–5:03 → D; 5:04–6:32 → C; 6:33–9:43 → B; 9:44–12:00 → A
O	0:10–0:23 → O; 0:24–0:36 → N; 0:37–0:51 → M; 0:52–1:07 → L; 1:08–1:24 → K; 1:25–1:43 → J; 1:44–2:04 → I; 2:05–2:29 → H; 2:30–2:58 → G; 2:59–3:33 → F; 3:34–4:17 → E; 4:18–5:16 → D; 5:17–6:44 → C; 6:45–9:54 → B; 9:55–12:00 → A
Z	0:10–0:22 → Z; 0:23–0:34 → O; 0:35–0:48 → N; 0:49–1:02 → M; 1:03–1:18 → L; 1:19–1:36 → K; 1:37–1:55 → J; 1:56–2:17 → I; 2:18–2:42 → H; 2:43–3:10 → G; 3:11–3:45 → F; 3:46–4:29 → E; 4:30–5:27 → D; 5:28–6:56 → C; 6:57–10:05 → B; 10:06–12:00 → A

TABLE 1-13 (1-8) SIMPLIFIED REPETITIVE DIVE TABLE

Depth (feet)	40	50	60	70	80	90	100	110	120	130	140	150	160	170	180	190
A	7	6	5	4	4	3	3	3	3	3	2	2	2	2	2	2
B	17	13	11	9	8	7	7	6	6	6	5	5	4	4	4	4
C	25	21	17	15	13	11	10	10	9	8	7	7	6	6	6	6
D	37	29	24	20	18	16	14	13	12	11	10	10	9	9	8	8
E	49	38	30	26	23	20	18	16	15	13	12	12	11	10	10	10
F	61	47	36	31	28	24	22	20	18	16	15	14	13	13	12	11
G	73	56	44	37	32	29	26	24	21	19	18	17	16	15	14	13
H	87	66	52	43	38	33	30	27	25	22	20	19	18	17	16	15
I	101	76	61	50	43	38	34	31	28	25	23	22	20	19	18	17
J	116	87	70	57	48	43	38	34	32	28	26	24	23	22	20	19
K	138	99	79	64	54	47	43	38	35	31	29	27	26	24	22	21
L	161	111	88	72	61	53	48	42	39	35	32	31	29	27	25	24
M	187	124	97	80	68	58	52	47	43	38	35	32	31	29	27	26
N	213	142	107	87	73	64	57	51	46	40	38	35	33	31	29	28
O	241	160	117	96	80	70	62	55	50	44	40	38	36	34	31	30
Z	257	169	122	100	84	73	64	57	52	46	42	40	37	35	32	31

NEW GROUPS

BLACK NUMBERS are "Residual Nitrogen Times"—time in minutes that a diver is to consider that he has already spent on the bottom when he starts a Repetitive Dive.

WHITE NUMBERS are bottom time limits in minutes for No Decompression Dives.

TABLE 1-10 (1-5) U.S. NAVY Standard Air Decompression Table. (Simplified for the Sport Diver)

Depth (feet)	Bottom Time (min)	Decompression stops (min) 20(ft)	10(ft)	Repetitive Group
40	200		0	(*)
	210		2	N
	230		7	N
50	100		0	(*)
	110		3	L
	120		5	M
	140		10	M
	160		21	N
60	60		0	(*)
	70		2	K
	80		7	L
	100		14	M
	120		26	N
	140		39	O
70	50		0	(*)
	60		8	K
	70		14	L
	80		18	M
	90		23	N
	100	2	33	N
	110	4	41	O
	120	6	47	O
	130		52	O
80	40		0	(*)
	50		10	K
	60		17	L
	70		23	M
	80	2	31	N
	90	7	39	N
	100	11	46	O
	110	13	53	O
90	30		0	(*)
	40		7	J
	50		18	L
	60	7	25	M
	70	13	30	N
	80	18	40	N
	90	48		O

Depth	Bottom Time	20(ft)	10(ft)	Repetitive Group
100	25		0	(*)
	30		3	K
	40		15	L
	50	2	24	N
	60	9	28	N
	70	17	39	O
110	20		0	(*)
	25		3	H
	30		7	J
	40	2	21	L
	50	8	26	M
	60	18	36	N
120	15		0	(*)
	20		2	H
	25		6	I
	30		14	K
	40	5	25	L
	50	15	31	N
130	10		0	(*)
	15		1	F
	20		4	H
	25		10	J
	30	3	18	M
	40	10	25	N
140	10		0	(*)
	15		2	G
	20		6	I
	25	2	14	J
	30	5	21	K
150	5		0	(*)
	10		1	C
	15		3	E
	20		7	G
	25		17	H
	30	8	24	K
160	5		0	(*)
	10		1	D
	15		4	F
	20		11	H
	25	3	20	K
170	5		0	D
	10		2	F
	15	2	5	H
	20	4	15	J
180	5		0	D
	10		3	F
	15	3	6	H
190	5		0	D
	10	1	3	G
	15	4	7	I

*See table 1-11 (1-6) for Repetitive Groups in "No Decompression Dives."

Dive Plan

DIVE	DEPTH	BOTTOM TIME	ARRIVAL TIME AT SURFACE	DEPARTURE TIME NEXT DIVE
1st				
2nd				
3rd				
4th				

INSTRUCTIONS FOR USE

For a "no decompression" dive:
1. Find the depth you have dived along the top of Table 1-11.
2. Drop down to the figure which denotes your Bottom Time.
3. Go across to the right to Table 1-12.
4. Follow the arrow upward until you find the time spent out of the water since the last dive (Surface Interval).
5. Go across to the right to find the allowable Bottom Time (white numbers) for the next dive. These are listed under the appropriate depths at the top of each column. The Black Numbers are "Residual Nitrogen Times" and are only important for figuring "Decompression" Dives.
6. If the "no decompression" limits are exceeded, go to Table 1-10 for Decompression stops and times.

Use of Table 1-10
a) All decompression stops are timed in minutes.
b) Ascent rate is 60 feet per minute.
c) The chest level of the diver should be maintained as close as possible to each decompression depth for the number of minutes listed.
d) The time at each stop is the exact time that is spent at that decompression depth.

DEFINITIONS:
1. Bottom time (in minutes) starts when the diver leaves the surface and ends only when the diver starts a direct ascent back to the surface. Always select the exact or next greater bottom time exposure.
2. Depth (in feet) The deepest depth of descent. Always enter the tables on the exact or next greater depth reached.
3. Residual Nitrogen Time—Time in minutes that a diver is to consider he has already spent on the bottom when he starts a repetitive dive.

PLAN YOUR DIVE—DIVE YOUR PLAN
Always carry the Dive Tables on a dive—they may save your life.

The "No Calculation Dive Tables" are a "simplified linear system for repetitive scuba dives," in which the U.S. Navy Dive Tables have been modified to make it easier to follow your bottom times, repetitive group letters, surface interval times, and residual nitrogen times through the tables. These tables also help you calculate your dive plans more quickly.

It cannot be stressed enough that **once you have planned your dive, dive strictly according to that plan.** Variations, even though they may be "just a few feet" or "just a few minutes" can place you in an entirely different repetitive group and could cause you to exceed your no-decompression limit at a certain depth. To be certain of your calculations during a dive, **always carry the tables with you and use them.**

Two examples for using the "No Calculation Dive Tables" follow.

Example—
Problem—A buddy team photographs various species of coral at 85 feet for 25 minutes. They rest on the surface for 1 hour and 20 minutes and then descend to 60 feet for 15 minutes to find some weights dropped from a previous dive. Determine their repetitive groups, residual nitrogen time (RNT), and total bottom time (TBT).

Solution—Find the depth in the top scale of Table 1-11 (No-Decompression Table). In this case, go to the next greater depth (90 feet). Read vertically down from 90 to find the bottom time (25 minutes). By reading horizontally either way on the same line, you find that the divers are in repetitive group "G" when they surface. Now enter table 1-12 (Surface Interval Credit Table) at letter "G" and read upwards in the column until you reach the two numbers their surface interval (1:20) falls between. Follow the arrow to the right in the same line to find their new group designation letter "E." By reading to the right and stopping under the depth of their second dive (60 feet) in Table 1-13 (Repetitive Dive Table), you find

that their residual nitrogen time (time in minutes to consider a diver has already spent on the bottom before a repetitive dive) is 30 minutes (black number). The white number (30) is the bottom time limit for no-decompression dives. By adding the RNT (30) and the actual bottom time (15), you find the buddy team has a TBT of 45 minutes. Now, go back to Table 1-11; under 60 feet you find that a 45-minute TBT puts the divers in repetitive group "H." If they decide to dive again, they will enter the tables as "H" divers.

Example—
Problem—Two divers descend along the anchor line until they reach the bottom at 80 feet. They survey the area and start their ascent 22 minutes later. They come to the surface, wait 45 minutes, and descend to 65 feet. They dive for 25 minutes at this depth. Determine their repetitive groups, their residual nitrogen time (RNT), total bottom time (TBT), and, if they would have to decompress, how long and at what depth.

Solution—Find the depth in the top scale of Table 1-11. Read vertically down from 80 to find the bottom time (22 minutes). Using the next highest time (25 minutes) you find that they become "F" divers after the first dive. By entering Table 1-12 at F and locating the surface interval of 45 minutes, you can also see that the divers remain "F" divers. Table 1-13 shows that "F" divers at 65 feet (70 feet) already have 31 minutes of residual nitrogen in their bodies. By adding the RNT (31) and the actual bottom time (25), you find the divers have a TBT of 56 minutes, which is 6 minutes over the no-decompression limit at the depth of 65 (70) feet. (See the top scale in Table 1-11.) Turn to Table 1-10 (Standard Air Decompression Table) and find the next greatest bottom time (60 minutes) beside the 70-foot depth. The two right-hand columns designate that the divers will have to decompress for 8 minutes at 10 feet and they will end up as "K" divers.

LOCATING YOUR NEAREST
RECOMPRESSION CHAMBER

The following numbers may be called 24 hours a day, seven days a week. Physicians are on call and consultation can be provided on air embolism or decompression sickness cases. Each maintains a world-wide listing of recompression chambers.

Brooks Air Force Base
LEO-FAST-Command Post
AC512-536-3278

U.S. Navy Experimental Diving Unit
EDU Duty Phone
AC904-234-4353

SAFE DIVING PRACTICES

Every dive can be a safe and interesting event if every effort is made to recognize and control the variables, and the greatest variable is you.

Know yourself completely. Learn exactly what you are capable of. Be absolutely honest in your appraisal of your condition. Be aware of the precise effects of drugs, or alcohol, and avoid them completely before diving. Smoking and diet also impose certain limits. Smoking, for instance, interferes with the body's ability to transfer oxygen. If you smoke, admit your reduced efficiency. Certain foods are definitely gas-producing; some people are affected more than others. Remember their effect and avoid those foods before diving or limit yourself accordingly.

Know your personal limitations and abide by them. If you have certain phobias, fatigue easily, or are overly susceptible to cold, admit it and plan accordingly and never overextend yourself. Don't try to match performance with people who have set no personal restrictions. Try to swim with a buddy who falls into your physical and skill categories.

Also, know your swimming fitness and knowledge limitations. Again, refrain from overextending yourself. Constantly strive to upgrade and improve all your skills. Practice emergency procedures with your buddy on every dive—don't wait for emergencies to happen. Stay current on the latest emergency procedures. Take courses in lifesaving, cardio-pulmonary resuscitation, and first aid.

Never dive without a buddy, and try to dive with a buddy you have practiced with many times; someone whom you know well enough to know their strong points, weaknesses, and probable reactions. Practice buddy breathing for at least a couple of minutes on every dive. Don't wait until an emergency occurs to find that you and your buddy have different conceptions of the proper way to handle these emergencies.

Preplan every dive no matter how short or insignificant it may appear to be. An essential of predive planning is a thorough equipment check. Don't dive with marginal equipment. There are enough unsuspected things that can happen without further complicating a situation with equipment malfunction.

Approach every dive with a positive and bright attitude. If you don't feel good about it, don't dive! A positive attitude promotes quick reactions; a negative attitude can slow the reactions considerably. Under stress, reactions can be warped enough without any other contributing factors being present.

Understand yourself, your equipment, and your environment to insure yourself of the maximum enjoyment of diving.

The following step-by-step summary of safe diving practices will help you quickly review these important points. Use the summary periodically to recall any forgotten details.

1. BE WELL TRAINED. Be trained in scuba diving by a certified instructor of scuba diving and certified by a nationally recognized certifying organization.

2. NEVER DIVE ALONE. Always dive with a buddy who is completely familiar with you and your diving practices.

3. NEVER HOLD YOUR BREATH WHILE USING SCUBA. Breathe regularly. Exhale during emergency ascents. Do not hyperventilate excessively before breath-hold dives.

4. DON'T DIVE BEYOND YOUR LIMITS. Maintain good mental and physical condition for diving. Only dive when feeling well. Do not use any intoxicating liquor or dangerous drug before diving. Have a regular medical examination for diving. Be sure to exercise regularly, keep well rested, and maintain a well-balanced diet.

5. **AVOID DEPTHS DEEPER THAN 100 FEET.** This is the recommended sport diving limit.

6. **USE PROPER EQUIPMENT.** Use correct, complete, and proper diving equipment which is checked before each dive and well-maintained. Do not loan your scuba equipment to a non-certified diver. Have your scuba equipment regularly serviced by a qualified person. When scuba diving in open water, use flotation equipment (vest or buoyancy compensator) and a submersible pressure gauge and/or reserve warning mechanism.

7. **PLAN YOUR DIVE.** Know the area. Establish emergency procedures. Know the limitations of yourself, your buddy, and your equipment. Use the best possible judgement and common sense in planning and setting the limitations of each dive, allowing a margin of safety in order to be prepared for emergencies. Set reasonable limits for depth and time in the water. Always buddy dive—know each other's equipment, know hand signals, and stay in contact.

8. **ALWAYS WEAR A BUOYANCY COMPENSATOR.** Control your buoyancy to make diving as easy as possible. Be prepared to ditch your weight belt, make an emergency ascent, buddy breathe, clear your mask and mouthpiece, or take other emergency action if needed. In an emergency: stop and think; get control; take action.

9. **PUT YOUR WEIGHT BELT ON LAST.** Ditch your weight belt when a potential emergency arises. Be sure to unclasp it completely and throw it well away from your body.

10. **USE A DIVER'S FLAG AND FLOAT.** Make sure that your diving area is well-identified to avoid potential hazards from boats in the area.

11. **HAVE YOUR TANKS VISUALLY INSPECTED AT LEAST ONCE A YEAR AND HYDROSTATICALLY TESTED EVERY FIVE YEARS.** The hydrostat test every five years is required by law, but a visual inspection every year can head off trouble before it happens.

12. **USE ONLY CLEAN, DRY, FILTERED AIR IN SCUBA TANKS.** Be sure any source of compressed air always meets established standards for diving air.

13. **NEVER USE EARPLUGS OR GOGGLES.** Air pressure squeezes can cause damage in any area that cannot be vented.

14. **DON'T CARRY KILLED GAME.** Killed game can attract creatures that can become aggressive when they sense food.

15. **CANCEL DIVES WHEN WATER AND WEATHER CONDITIONS ARE QUESTIONABLE.** Too many unknowns can happen without aggravating the situation. It is far better to have everything in your favor which will make emergencies less serious.

16. **BE FAMILIAR WITH THE AREA.** Know your diving location. Avoid dangerous places and poor conditions. Take whatever special precautions are required.

17. **ASCEND PROPERLY.** When surfacing, look up and around, move slowly and listen, hold your hand up if any possible hazards exist. Do not hold your breath with scuba. Be sure to equalize pressure early and often both during ascent and descent.

18. **KNOW DECOMPRESSION PROCEDURES.** Be familiar with decompression tables and emergency procedures. Make all possible dives "no-decompression" dives. Avoid stage decompression particularly on repetitive dives, at altitude, or when flying after the dive.

19. **DON'T OVEREXTEND YOURSELF.** If you are cold, tired, injured, out of air, or not feeling well, get out of the water. Diving is no longer fun or safe. If any abnormality persists, get medical attention.

20. **AVOID TOUCHING UNKNOWN CREATURES UNDER WATER.** Be especially careful of anything very beautiful or very ugly.

21. **KNOW YOUR BOAT AND REGULATIONS.** Be sure any boat used for diving is legally and adequately equipped for diving.

22. **BE A GOOD CITIZEN DIVER AND SPORTSMAN.** Comply with laws and regulations concerning diving. Be friendly and respect personal property. When diving have your certification card, diving log, and identification nearby.

23. **BE AN ACTIVE DIVER.** Keep actively diving and logging your dives with your buddy's signature by each logged dive. Try to dive no less than 12 times per year.

24. **CONTINUE YOUR TRAINING.** Continue your scuba diving training by taking advanced, open water, or specialty courses.

EQUIPMENT CHECKLIST

DIVING EQUIPMENT

_____ SWIM SUIT
_____ MASK & ANTI-FOG SOLUTION
_____ SNORKEL & KEEPER
_____ FINS
_____ WET SUIT
  _____ JACKET
  _____ BOOTS
  _____ GLOVES
  _____ PANTS
  _____ VEST
  _____ HOOD
_____ WEIGHT BELT & WEIGHTS
_____ BUOYANCY COMPENSATOR
_____ FULL SCUBA TANK & BACKPACK
_____ REGULATOR
_____ SUBMERSIBLE PRESSURE GAUGE
_____ WATCH
_____ DEPTH GAUGE
_____ COMPASS
_____ DECOMPRESSION TABLES
_____ DIVER'S FLAG/FLOAT &
      ANCHOR/LINE
_____ WHISTLE
_____ KNIFE
_____ LOGBOOK & PENCIL
_____ GEAR BAG

OTHER ITEMS

_____ DRY CLOTHES
_____ TOWELS
_____ FOOD & DRINKING WATER
_____ SUNGLASSES
_____ SUNTAN LOTION
_____ LOGBOOK
_____ CERTIFICATION CARD
_____ SPORT DIVING MANUAL

SPECIALTY EQUIPMENT

_____ DECOMPRESSION COMPUTER
_____ THERMOMETER
_____ EMERGENCY FLARE
_____ LIGHT & BATTERIES
_____ SLATE & PENCIL
_____ SAFETY LINE (200 FT.)
_____ BUDDY LINE (6 FT.)

_____ LIFT BAG
_____ PHOTOGRAPHY EQUIPMENT
  _____ FLASH
  _____ CAMERA
  _____ FILM
  _____ FLASHBULBS
  _____ BATTERIES
_____ SPEARFISHING GEAR
  _____ SPEAR
  _____ FISHING LICENSE
  _____ GAME BAG

SPARE PARTS & REPAIR KIT

_____ MASK STRAP & BUCKLE
_____ FIN STRAP & BUCKLE
_____ "O" RINGS
_____ CO_2 CARTRIDGES
_____ REGULATOR HIGH PRESSURE PLUG
_____ SILICONE SPRAY OR GREASE
_____ WET SUIT CEMENT
_____ NEEDLE & THREAD
_____ EXTRA MASK LENS
_____ WATERPROOF PLASTIC TAPE
_____ PLIERS
_____ WRENCH
_____ SCREWDRIVER
_____ SMALL KNIFE
_____ BUOYANCY VEST PATCHES

FIRST AID KIT

_____ ADHESIVE TAPE
_____ ALCOHOL SOLUTION (70%)
_____ AMMONIA SOLUTION
_____ ANTISEPTIC SPRAY
_____ ADHESIVE STRIPS
_____ BUTTERFLY CLOSURES
_____ COMPRESSES
_____ COTTON SWABS
_____ RAZOR BLADE
_____ SCISSORS
_____ SNAKEBITE KIT
_____ SPLINTS
_____ SOAP
_____ SEASICK PILLS
_____ DIMES & EMERGENCY PHONE NUMBERS
_____ BAKING SODA
_____ NASAL DECONGESTANT

index

a

ACCIDENT, 3-10, 6-8, 6-9, 6-10,
  6-20, 6-21, 7-3, 8-5
ACTIVITY, 5-13, 5-22
ADDITIONAL TRAINING, 6-14
AFT, 3-6
AGE, 6-5
AGONIC LINE, 4-12
AIR
  embolism, 7-26
  leaks, 8-5
  pressure, 4-26
  supply, 1-20, 2-22, 6-4,
    6-8, 8-2
  surface-supplied, 2-22
AIR CONSUMPTION, 4-25, 5-13,
  8-4, 8-5
  rate, 1-19
  table, 4-25
ALCOHOL, 3-13, 8-7, 8-8, 8-24
ALGAE, 5-6
ALTITUDE TABLE, 8-28
AMBIENT PRESSURE, 1-22
AMERICAN HEART ASSOCIA-
  TION, 7-25
ANCHOR, 3-6, 3-9, 3-10
  3-16 through 3-20, 3-22, 3-24,
  3-26, 3-29 through 3-31, 5-21
  line, 3-20, 3-22, 5-9, 6-19,
  8-14, 8-15, 8-28
ANCHORAGE, 4-22
ANIMALS, 5-14
ARTIFICAL RESPIRATION, 7-4,
  7-10, 7-12, 7-13, 7-17, 7-19,
  7-20, 7-23, 7-26, 7-27, 8-18
ASCENT, 2-24, 3-18, 5-10, 5-11,
  6-7, 6-8, 6-11, 6-15, 7-12,
  7-13, 7-18, 8-5, 8-15, 8-24
  buoyant, 6-18, 7-6
  direct, 8-24
  emergency, 6-10
  line, 5-20

ASCENT, (continued)
  normal, 6-18
  rate, 5-10, 5-21
ASSIST, 7-19
  buddy, 7-8, 7-10
ASSOCIATIONS
  instructor, 3-10
AUDIBLE RESERVE, 1-21
AUXILIARY LIGHT, 5-20, 5-21

b

BACKPACK, 1-11, 1-13
  maintenance, 1-14
BACK ROLL, 3-31
BALANCED REGULATOR, 1-15
BARRACUDA, 6-7
BATTERY PACK, 5-17
BAY, 5-15
BEACH LANDING, 3-32
BEHAVIOR, 6-10, 6-22
BELT
  weight, 1-9, 1-14, 3-18, 3-31,
    4-29, 5-16, 6-7, 7-5, 8-14
BENDS, 8-16, 8-28
BEZEL, 1-25, 4-8, 4-10, 4-11, 4-15
BILGE, 3-6
BIOLUMINESCENCE, 5-15
BLEEDING, 7-26
BLOOD, 7-24
  flow, 8-17
  pressure, 6-10, 6-15
BOAT, 3-20, 3-32, 7-19
  cabin cruiser, 3-5
  commercial, 3-4, 3-6, 3-27
  converted, 3-5
  crew, 3-14
  dive, 3-3, 3-6, 3-18, 3-23,
    3-24, 3-28
  diving, 3-1 through 3-32
  equipment, 3-9
  fishing, 3-4
  inflated, 3-5

BOAT, (continued)
  license, 3-8, 3-9
  parts of, 3-6
  private, 3-5, 3-24
  procedure, 3-5, 3-14, 3-24
  selecting, 3-27
  small, 3-32
  sail, 3-5
  sports fishing, 3-4
  trip checklist, 3 11
  yacht, 3-5
BOATING, 3-27
BOARD-MOUNTED COMPASS,
  4-10, 4-11
BOOTS
  wet suit, 5-16, 8-6
BOTTOM, 3-22, 3-23, 5-9, 5-10,
  5-11, 5-15, 5-20, 5-21, 6-18,
  6-21, 8-14, 8-15
BOTTOM TIME, 2-20, 2-21,
  8-24, 8-26
BOTTOM TIMER, 8-11,
  8-24, 8-26
BOUNCE DIVE, 8-28
BOW, 3-6, 3-7, 3-22
BRACKET LINE, 4-15
BREASTBONE, 7-24
BREATHING, 6-13, 6-15,
  6-17, 7-26
  effort, 1-15
  rate, 6-17
  resistance, 1-5, 1-15, 8-5
BUBBLE, 3-19, 8-14, 8-15, 8-25
  formation, 8-17
BUDDY, 1-26, 3-11, 3-14, 3-16,
  3-18, 3-22, 3-24, 3-31, 5-9,
  5-12, 5-16, 5-19, 5-22, 7-3,
  7-4, 7-7, 8-9, 8-13 through 8-16
  assist, 7-8, 7-10
  assistance, 3-18
  breathing, 2-24
  breathing ascent, 6-18
  check, 3-18, 8-12, 8-13
  diving, 6-19, 6-20
  line, 6-20